Willie McCarney was born in Wales but grew up in Northern Ireland. His father encouraged him to embrace education as a way out of poverty. He passed the 11+, studied hard and graduated as a teacher in 1961. He was firmly of the view that every child should be given the chance to be educated to the limits of his/her talents. When The Troubles, broke out in August 1969 he was teaching in St Peter's Secondary School in West Belfast, literally in the eye of the storm. Seemingly oblivious to the guerrilla war raging around him, he set out to promote the rights of disaffected young people in St Peter's. He never dreamt that his project would grow into an international, worldwide, campaign for the rights of all children.

To my good friend, John Hume, the Architect of the Northern Ireland peace process; and to Fr Alec Reid of Clonard Monastery, who enabled the talks to begin; To Dr Fred Milson, Methodist Minister, Principal Lecturer and Head of Department at Westhill College, Birmingham, who devoted his life to promoting the best interests of children and young people, for supporting my efforts to protect the best interest of children in West Belfast as a guerrilla war raged around us. To all the men and women around the world who carry on a never-ending struggle defending the Rights of the Child. To my sister Una, my principal carer, who is always at my side, offering a helping hand when I am down, ensuring that the path ahead is free of obstacles; To my son, Liam, for his encouragement and support in all that I do.

Willie McCarney

DICING WITH DEATH

AUSTIN MACAULEY PUBLISHERS®
LONDON * CAMBRIDGE * NEW YORK * SHARJAH

A CIP catalogue record for this title is available from the British Library.

ISBN 9781035880461 (Paperback)
ISBN 9781035880478 (ePub e-book)

www.austinmacauley.com

First Published 2024
Austin Macauley Publishers Ltd®
1 Canada Square
Canary Wharf
London
E14 5AA

I am indebted to my sister, Una, and my son, Liam, for commenting on the early drafts, and for drawing my attention to things I had left out. They were also meticulous in their proofreading. I would like to thank my good friends, Tom McGonigle, Tommy Fee and Paddy Mooney (RIP) for providing valuable feedback on earlier drafts. I offer my condolences to Paddy's wife and son on his sudden and untimely death. A special word of thanks to, Mary Toland, for the speed with which she carried out the proofreading and for her attention to detail in spotting other errors where the text was factually incorrect or where someone's name had not been altered.

Table of Contents

A Synopsis — 11

Chapter 1: The Origin of the Troubles in Northern Ireland — 15

Chapter 2: New Boy on the Block — 20

Chapter 3: Living for Ireland — 34

Chapter 4: The IRA Campaign 1956–57 — 39

Chapter 5: At Crossroads — 46

Caught in Possession of Pondweed — 49

A Case of Road Rage — 50

The Case of the Missing Loaves — 51

One Turn too Many — 53

Chapter 6: St Peter's Secondary School and the Tripartite System of Streaming Children — 55

Chapter 7: We Need to Listen to, and Value, Each Child — 63

Chapter 8: The Abominable 'No!' Man — 72

Chapter 9: The Civil Rights Campaign—
       Caledon 1968   76

Chapter 10: In the Eye of the Storm   82

Chapter 11: Dicing with Death   88

Chapter 12: Skating on Thin Ice   101

Chapter 13: ROSLA Highlighted the
       Need for Change   123

Chapter 14: Knowing When to Walk Away   128

Chapter 15: Any Irishman Will Do   132

Chapter 16: 33 Years As a Lay Magistrate   147

Chapter 17: Spreading the Word   168

Chapter 18: No Escaping the Troubles   174

Chapter 19: It Just Grow'd   183

A Synopsis

Dr Willie McCarney outlines his experience of living and teaching in West Belfast throughout *The Troubles* (a period of urban guerrilla warfare) in Northern Ireland. He sets the context by explaining that *The Troubles* originated in the partitioning of Ireland by the British under the terms of the Government of Ireland Act, 1920. Northern Ireland was deliberately set up with an inbuilt two-thirds Protestant majority. From its creation in 1921, the Roman Catholic minority community suffered discrimination and was politically marginalised, under the Unionist and wholly Protestant government.

Willie was born in Wales but grew up in a strongly Republican area of Northern Ireland. Popular ballads ensured that the celebrated oath sworn at McArt's Fort atop Cave Hill, overlooking Belfast, by the leaders of the 1798 rebellion: 'Never to desist in our efforts until we have subverted the authority of England over our country and asserted our independence' remained fresh in everyone's mind. At a subliminal level, the ballads glorify the act of dying for Ireland. They offer young people the opportunity to become tomorrow's heroes and martyrs.

Willie wanted to encourage young people to live for Ireland. Following the IRA Campaign 1956–57, he decided to become a teacher and promote the best interests of children and young people. When *The Troubles* broke out in August 1969, he was teaching in St Peter's Secondary School in West Belfast, literally in the eye of the storm.

While there was terrorist-related activity happening somewhere in Northern Ireland daily, Belfast bore the brunt of it and the two-mile stretch of road between his home and the school had more than its share. Willie travelled that corridor of death to and from school every day. In school, he was prepared to put his life on the line protecting the rights of disaffected young people. He tried to keep the older boys out of the arms of the IRA, who would recruit them into the Fianna (Junior IRA), and out of reach of the security forces who would arrest them for petty crimes and then release them on condition that they became informers.

Willie was ready to protect them against all comers. He walked the middle ground, neither on one side nor the other. The police and the soldiers were professionals. They could look after themselves. He did not support the IRA, nor take orders from them, nor allow himself to be used by them. He saw his role as protecting the young people in his care. He was walking on quicksand, knowing that if he put a foot wrong, he could vanish without a trace.

Andersonstown, where he lived, and Ballymurphy, where he taught, were both no-go areas for the security forces. After *Operation Motorman*, St Peters was taken over by a company of *the Parachute Regiment*. The IRA announced that the school was now a legitimate target. The teaching staff announced that they and the pupils were withdrawing from the school and would not return until the army vacated it.

Willie's main concern throughout this period was how quickly murder and mayhem became the norm. It was 'normal' to have to skirt around the burnt-out remains of buses, lorries, and cars—the debris of the previous night's rioting—or to make detours to avoid suspect bombs on the way to and from work. The most disconcerting aspect for him was that death and destruction became so commonplace that incidents were quickly forgotten. People got on with living—after they had buried their dead.

The focus in *Dicing with Death* is on his efforts to promote the rights of disaffected young people in St Peter's Secondary School. But he tells us that this is only half the story. Seemingly oblivious to the guerrilla war raging around him, Willie went to unprecedented lengths to promote the best interests of children and young people in general and of disaffected youth in particular. He set out to promote the rights of disaffected young people in St Peter's Secondary School in West Belfast but saw his project grow into an international, worldwide, campaign for the rights of all children. When asked to explain how this happened, he replied like Topsy, "It just grow'd."

He was elected chair of the Northern Ireland Association of Lay Magistrates, then Chair of the British Association and, finally, President of the International Association. He was regarded as an expert on children's rights and his services were in demand, not only by many governments but also by organisations such as the UN Development Programme, the Council of Europe and UNICEF. There was a continuous flow of requests for him to get involved in a range of projects as well as requests from various countries to present papers at seminars.

Dicing with Death provides a frank and honest insight into the life and career, and the remarkable achievements, of a professional living and working in the unique environment of West Belfast throughout a prolonged period of guerrilla warfare.

Chapter 1
The Origin of the Troubles in Northern Ireland

Northern Ireland became a political entity in 1921 under the terms of the Government of Ireland Act, 1920, when Britain carved it off from the rest of Ireland. To appease the Ulster Protestants, who had declared their intention in 1912 to resist Home Rule by force of arms, if necessary, six of Ulster's nine counties were partitioned off. This segment of Ireland would be known as 'Northern Ireland' and would remain under British control. The remaining 26 counties would be known as the Irish Free State, which was granted dominion status, i.e., it would be a self-governing territory of the then British Empire.

Since then, the two parts of Ireland have grown further apart. The feeling of insecurity on the part of the settlers noted in the seventeenth century following the Plantation of Ulster, and the 'siege mentality' which ensued, was clear in the aftermath of the partition. Catholics were attacked and driven from their homes and places of work. The IRA launched a counter-offensive designed to undermine the authority of the 'new government' and prevent it from functioning effectively. The new government of Northern Ireland declared itself to be 'a Protestant Parliament for a Protestant People'. Representatives of the Catholic minority were consigned to the role of permanent opposition with no prospects of exercising political power. It is hardly surprising that Nationalist members refused initially to take their seats, while other members of the minority refused to participate in the 'public' life of the state, for partition ignored the presence and aspirations of approximately one-third of its inhabitants and 75% of the whole island.

The South advanced from dominion status, through the Constitution of 1937, to formally become a Republic in 1949 and leave the Commonwealth. The Constitution of 1937, to some extent, enshrined Catholic social teaching (e.g. divorce was outlawed). Article 44 (repealed thirty-five years later) recognised the special position of the Catholic Church within the state. The confessional influences increased Unionist fears and retrospectively seemed to them to justify their belief that Home Rule would have led to Rome Rule.

In addition, Article 2 of the Irish Constitution says: 'The national territory consists of the whole island of Ireland, its islands and the territorial seas'. Article 3 says: 'Pending the re-integration of the national territory, and without prejudice to the right of the Parliament and government established by this Constitution to exercise jurisdiction over the whole of that territory, the laws enacted by that Parliament shall have the like area and extent of application as the laws of Saorstat Eireann[1] and the like extra-territorial effect'. In the view of Ulster Unionists, Articles 2 & 3 served to encourage the

---

[1] *Saorstat Eireann*—the Irish Free State

various IRA factions in their attempt to reunite Ireland by violent means. Hence the pressure to have them repealed following the 1998 Good Friday Agreement.

Three further factors seemed to reinforce partition. The South remained neutral during the Second World War, while the North of Ireland played a substantial part. Secondly, British Government financial transfers (particularly after 1945) to Northern Ireland supported a welfare state and an education system which could not be maintained in the South. The economic 'miracle' in the Republic, coinciding with the accession to the premiership of Sean Lemass in 1959 altered this considerably, but not totally. Thirdly, the marked decline of the Protestant population in the South (partly due to mixed marriages) seemed to suggest to Protestants that there was no future in being a minority in a Catholic-dominated state.

In the North, the pattern of a de facto Protestant domination and Catholic dissociation from the state continued, in essence, undisturbed until 1968. The Civil Rights Movement broke the old mould because it began as a demand for civil rights within the state rather than the traditional nationalist or republican demand for its abolition. It was led by a new generation of university-educated Catholics, of whom John Hume is the best-known on the international scene.

The voting system as it existed at that time meant that homeowners (mainly Protestants) had votes in local elections, while owners of businesses (mainly Protestants) had multiple votes; people living in rented accommodation (mainly Catholics) had no votes. This meant that many Catholics were disenfranchised, and Protestants were always going to have a majority in any local election. The Civil Rights Movement called for 'One man one vote'.

Housing was another hot issue. To ensure that voting patterns would always favour Protestants, Catholics were kept in crowded conditions, with multiple families sharing the same home. Young married couples were forced to live with their parents, finding it impossible to get a home of their own. Young Protestant couples had no such worries. The civil rights campaign called for a fair allocation of housing.

Regarding employment, Catholics were $2^1/_2$ times more likely than Protestants to be unemployed. The Civil Rights Movement called for a fair allocation of jobs. The movement also called for the abolition of the B-Specials (the part-time police force which was 100% Protestant and perceived as being militantly anti-Catholic) and reform of the regular police force, which was about 93% Protestant.

The Northern Ireland government did all in its power to stamp out the Civil Rights Movement. Some members of the Protestant Community reacted violently to what they perceived as a threat to their position. 1969 saw attacks by Protestant mobs, many accompanied by members of the B-Specials, and occasionally by members of the regular police force, on Catholic homes and property which were torched in Belfast and Derry. Something in the region of 93,000 people, mainly Catholics, were driven from their homes. Finally, the British Government was forced to intervene, and the British army was ordered to move into Belfast and Derry in 1969 to protect Catholic homes and property from the Protestant onslaughts.

The harsh way in which the government dealt with the Civil Rights Movement and its leaders in the early days, followed by the pogroms of 1969, left a feeling of resentment amongst Catholics which persisted even after most of the aims were achieved—equal voting rights for all local, as well as Westminster, elections, the re-organisation of the police, the replacement of the B-Specials, the transfer of housing from local councils to a central authority, the introduction of procedures for dealing with complaints against statutory bodies and the establishment of a Fair Employment Agency (now Commission). At the same time, the granting of these rights to Catholics was perceived by many Protestants as an undermining of their rights. Old divisions and animosities were refuelled.

Chapter 2
New Boy on the Block

My parents came from County Tyrone, Northern Ireland. Jobs were hard to come by and emigration was all that lay in store for many young Catholic men growing up at that time. My father's brother, Paddy, joined the British army and served for some years in Egypt and in India. Another brother, Ted, went to Wales and got a job with JL Eve Construction Company Ltd. erecting steel towers for high-tension electric cables. He fell off one of the towers and injured his back. His wife, Sarah, decided that she, and their three children, should go to Wales to be with him.

Sarah was my mother's sister, and they were very close. They had married the two brothers (my dad and Ted) and were inseparable. If Sarah was going to Wales, my mother was going too. It seemed like a sensible idea since my father could get full-time employment, while there was only casual work at home.

Sarah, with her three children and my parents, with their three children (almost identical in age to their cousins) set off for North Wales. The two families got adjoining houses in Maesgeirchen. Maesgeirchen, at that time, was a village not far from Bangor. While it still retains its name, it was swallowed up long ago by Bangor's urban sprawl.

Aunt Sarah was not keen that Ted should return to erecting pylons. Luckily, at that time, another job opportunity arose as work was about to commence on repairs to the Menai Bridge. The Menai Suspension Bridge joins the island of Anglesey to the mainland of Wales. The bridge was completed in 1826. Over the years, the 4.5 ton weight limit proved problematic for the increasing freight industry and in 1938 work began to replace the original wrought iron chains with steel ones. My father and Uncle Ted found employment on this project which lasted for about two years.

I was born in Maesgeirchen on 31 August 1938, a little over a year after my parents settled there. Aunt Sarah had a new baby the following year, 1939, a baby boy whom they christened Michael. I don't remember Michael. I was just over one year old. He was, by all accounts, a beautiful, bouncing baby. Mother and baby were in the local hospital; Michael in the baby unit downstairs and my aunt with the nursing mothers, upstairs. The babies would be brought up to the mums at feeding time and returned to the unit afterwards.

One day just after the nurse left the ward with Michael, Sarah heard a loud thump. She was not aware that anything untoward had happened, but when she saw Michael the next day, he was a very different baby—listless and unresponsive. The suspicion was that the nurse had either dropped Michael or banged his head on the bannisters on the way downstairs. But this could never be proven. In any event, Michael lived for just under a year and died on 26 February 1940. The cause of death was recorded as 'broncho pneumonia'.

In our family, the children were born almost exactly two years apart. Joseph was born in 1932, Eddie in 1934, Paddy in 1936, I was born in 1938 and Mary was born in 1940. Our birthdays were all in the summer months. Right on cue, my mother was pregnant again and a baby brother, Michael, was born on 28 November 1942. I never got to meet my new brother. He only survived for two hours after birth and never came home from the hospital. The cause of death was recorded as 'premature birth'.

Aunt Sarah's baby daughter, Margaret, was born in May 1941. She died on 25 April 1943, aged just 23 months—cause of death 'bronchial pneumonia'. Margaret was a very happy, and, apparently, very healthy, little girl. Her sudden death at just under two years of age was totally unexpected and hit Sarah and Ted very hard.

The blow was particularly hard to take because Sarah was pregnant again and had just received some very bad news. The doctors had diagnosed severe stomach pain as appendicitis and advised that an operation was essential, or Sarah could die. Sarah and Ted were presented with a dilemma. If the doctors didn't operate, Sarah would probably die, but if they did operate, Sarah was likely to lose her baby. Sarah was not prepared to risk the baby's life, especially since she had already lost two children—Michael and Margaret.

Sarah said that, if she was going to die, she wanted to die in Ireland. Ted said they would leave for home immediately. Of course, my mother wouldn't let her go alone. Both families packed their belongings and caught the ferry for Belfast on the way back to Co Tyrone. I was not yet five years old. We were going to stay with my mother's sister, Aunt Roseanne, in a large two-storey house where she lived with her husband,

Henry, and daughter, Mary. My aunt's house was big by local standards but not really intended for the crowd which now arrived. There were seven in my family and five in Aunt Sarah's—12 additional bodies to be fed and bedded down.

We left Wales in June 1943 because Sarah said she wanted to die in Ireland. She didn't have long to wait—she passed away four months later, on 26 October 1943. She was just 37 years old. Everyone was devastated. But the hardest hit were Uncle Ted and his three children—and my mum. My mum never got over Aunt Sarah's death.

Uncle Ted had arranged for his two daughters to start school in Omagh in September, and they stayed with friends in the town. This eased the pressure somewhat on Aunt Roseanne. After Aunt Sarah's death, he got a job in Newtownards and moved there with his three children.

My father found a house to rent not too far away. It was about half a mile away as the crow flies—down to the bottom of the glen, across a small river and up through the hazel woods. It must have been a great relief to my aunt when the seven members of my family moved out and into our new home in 'Glen Upper'. It was such a relief for us, as it must have been for my aunt, that we now had a house to ourselves.

But we did not get off to an auspicious start to life in our new home. My mum, who was pregnant again, took ill and was rushed into hospital because of concerns that she was going to lose her baby. She gave birth to a baby girl on 16 October 1944. She decided to call her 'Ann'. I was never to see my baby sister. Ann only survived for three hours—the cause of death was 'premature birth'. My mum became ill and, from then on, she needed support all day every day.

My mum's trauma continued. Her brother Peter, the youngest of her siblings, was a carpenter. He was working on a ship in Liverpool when he fell and was seriously injured. He died on 28 October 1945. Her mum died less than two weeks later, on 9 November 1945.

Our new home didn't have the amenities we had enjoyed in Wales—there was no running water, no flush toilet and the nearest shop was about a mile away. But the green rolling fields, the tall trees, the hazel woods, and the rippling stream flowing through the glen were more than enough compensation for me.

Our new landlord was Robert—a farmer who lived with his wife and two grown-up children across a couple of fields from our new home. Robert was not just a good landlord. He was a good neighbour as well. He told my father that we could cut firewood from the local hazelwood and asked only that my father manage the cutting so that no area was left denuded, and no gaps were left in fences. And he gave us two drills in one of his fields to grow potatoes and vegetables.

When we came to live in Glen Upper, Robert still kept some of his cows in a byre at the side of our house. His daughter, Julie, would be over every morning and every evening to tend to the cattle. She was a young woman in her early twenties. She was big and strong and could throw sacks of potatoes onto the tractor with hardly any effort. I used to watch out for her coming so that I could 'help' her. She would always give me a piggyback before she headed back home.

I seldom saw Robert's son Steven. I think he had a job in a local quarry, so he was seldom about during the day. I never saw any of the family at Mass on Sunday and asked my father about it. He told me that they didn't come to Mass on Sunday because they were not Catholics. 'Not being a Catholic' didn't mean a lot to me—apart from not seeing my neighbours on a Sunday morning. They were such nice people that I expected to see them every day and wondered why Sunday was different. Some years later, I heard that Steven had married a Catholic but don't know where he settled down. Marrying a Catholic in those days was regarded, by the Protestant community, as an act of treason. Steven was disinherited and the farm passed to his sister Julie.

I started school in Wales and had just completed my first year when my family moved back to Co Tyrone. It was time to continue my schooling. The school was in Loughmacrory, some three miles away if we took a shortcut through the meadows, using the stepping stones to get over the river. The river was little more than a gently flowing stream most of the time. But following heavy rain, it could become a raging torrent and we would have to make a long detour which nearly doubled our journey.

In 1948, we moved to a larger house in Loughmacrory. This house would be more convenient for us as it was less than half a mile from the school and the church. Once again, things did not get off to a good start. My mother never really recovered after Ann's birth. She died a few months after our move to Loughmacrory. The cause of death was 'Arteriosclerosis'. She was just 38. I was four months short of my tenth birthday.

Loughmacrory, like Glen Upper, is in the Parish of Carrickmore and the vast majority of families are Catholic. I was only aware of one Protestant family in Glen Upper, our landlord Henry's family. When we moved to Loughmacrory, we found that, once again, our closest neighbours were a

Protestant family who lived about a quarter of a mile from us. As in Glen Upper, we couldn't have asked for better neighbours. The children in both Protestant families were grown up except for Sam in Loughmacrory who was the same age as me. He was the only Protestant in our school. We were all jealous of him because he was allowed to come late every day. He didn't have to attend morning prayers or religious instruction.

I got on very well with him. I taught him to play handball. He was exceptionally good. Unfortunately, tournaments were generally held on a Sunday and the family didn't want their son to participate in sport on the Sabbath Day. I thought that if they knew how good he was, they might reconsider. I went and had a chat with his father, and he gave Sam permission to play in one tournament where he did exceptionally well. However, Sam told me he didn't want to upset his parents and that he had decided to give up handball.

Just across the field from our house, between the house and the lake, lay the estate of Sir John Roe, a member of the landed gentry and the Queen's representative in Tyrone. The estate was not Sir John's main residence. He spent most of his time in his main estate some miles away in Ballygawley. The Loughmacrory estate had suffered a bit from the US army occupation in 1944/45 and the grounds had been neglected since then. My paternal grandfather had come to live with us when he retired from his role as a gardener on an estate in Sixmilecross. One day, Sir John was out for a walk with his wife and as he passed our house, he noted how my grandfather had turned what used to be a wilderness into a flourishing vegetable garden. Sir John asked him if he would be prepared to try to do something with the gardens at his lodge. My grandfather agreed and because it was a major task, we were recruited from time to time to help him.

There was some friction between Sir John and the local populace, especially during the grouse-shooting season. Sir John would arrange a shoot and invite members of the gentry and high-ranking army officers from Omagh and surrounding districts. The local men were invited to act as beaters but sometimes, they would bring their shotguns with them and join in the shoot. The members of the gentry would not be best pleased, but being vastly outnumbered; they would just have to 'thole' it[2].

Sir John would not allow anyone to trespass on his land which bordered the lake. But he made an exception for us because we often helped our grandfather in the gardens. I always spoke to him as I would to any of my neighbours and did not treat him as a member of the 'hated British Establishment'. He allowed me to take a shortcut through the woods which surrounded his house, on the way to the lake. I once found a family of baby hedgehogs in a disused garden at the side of his house. I spotted my first otter swimming in the river which entered the lake a short distance away. But my fondest memory is of two baby long-eared owls which had just fledged and were sitting side by side on a branch close to their nest. I reached up to touch them and one of them grasped my finger tightly in its talons as if trying to frighten me away. Or perhaps he was just shaking hands! Those baby owls had the most beautiful brown eyes I had ever seen. The image in my mind is as clear today as it was then.

____

[2] From Ulster-Scots meaning they would just have to put up with it.

When we settled in, I learned that there was another Protestant family who lived about half a mile away. Their children were grown up and long past primary school age. One of the sons lived in the Gate Lodge of Sir John's estate and worked as a security man.

While there was some friction between the locals and Sir John, there was no real animosity towards him or any of the small number of Protestants who lived in the parish. The only comment I heard was: 'They are grand neighbours—just a wee bit odd around the Twelfth[3]'.

There was little focus on history in our primary school so there was no discussion about the Battle of the Boyne or the many rebellions since. But Ireland's is a singing culture, full of songs about valour and sacrifice and suffering with rousing and memorable ballads that fuel nationalism.

In those days, before TV and local cinemas, people used to Céili[4] in local houses. This was especially common when someone had family members home from America, or even from Scotland. They would throw a party. The general rule was that girls had to be invited but boys were always

---

[3].On 12 July (The Twelfth) each year, Ulster Protestants/loyalists/Orangemen celebrate the victory of the Protestant King William of Orange over the Catholic King James II at the Battle of the Boyne in 1690 which ensured a Protestant Ascendancy in Ireland.

[4] A céilí or cèilidh, is a social visit to a neighbour's house in Ireland (or Scotland). It may be one or two people calling in for a chat; a number of people coming to enjoy singing, dancing and playing Gaelic folk music; or it could be a much larger group meeting in a church hall, community centre or dance hall.

welcome—on one condition. The condition was that they should be prepared to contribute to the night's entertainment.

I remember once when a group of boys from Mountfield, who were notorious for starting fights, arrived at a party in Uncle Peter Ned's. The party, which was in full swing, was totally disrupted once the fighting started. I still remember my uncle's words as he related how this crowd had ruined the night's craic—'A pack of qualified moochers[5] who could neither sing, dance nor play music. They came to obstruct and obstruct they done'.

Songs commemorating heroes and martyrs were always popular at these parties. 'The Rising of the Moon' would ensure that the celebrated oath sworn at McArt's Fort atop Cave Hill, overlooking Belfast, by the leaders of the 1798 rebellion: 'Never to desist in our efforts until we have subverted the authority of England over our country and asserted our independence' remained fresh in everyone's mind. The words of 'God save Ireland!' are so memorable and the refrain so catchy that everybody could join in.

At a subliminal level, the ballads glorify the act of dying for Ireland. They offer young people the opportunity to become tomorrow's heroes and martyrs. They should be ready at a moment's notice to answer the call: 'Heads erect, eyes front, stepping proudly together' and they should be 'ready to die with a smile'. They were promised that God would be with them—'For freedom comes from God's right hand'.

---

[5] A moocher is someone who is always trying to get something for nothing—without giving anything in return

It appeared to me that this was a very effective propaganda stream and I even found myself being swept along, thinking that it would be nice to die for Ireland. As I moved through grammar school, I had more opportunities to read about the various rebellions. The reading raised questions—one big question in particular. What was the point of a group of young people queuing up to die? How was that going to benefit Mother Ireland? I had also come to realise that young people weren't just being asked to die for Ireland. They were being asked to kill for Ireland—something I could never countenance.

At this time, a Christian Brother arrived at our school to teach us Irish history. As it turned out, he taught his own version of it. His focus was Irish history, but there was no mention of ancient history—of the Neolithic tombs such as Newgrange, of the Tuatha De Danann or the coming of the Celts, St Patrick, Tara and the High Kings, the Viking invasions. His focus was on the conflict with England. Even then he didn't mention that the English first got a foothold in Ireland when Dermot MacMurrough offered to become a vassal to the King, Henry II, in return for military aid in retaking his kingdom (the Kingdom of Leinster).

Our historian began with Cromwell and his campaign to send the Irish 'To Hell or to Connacht'. He went into graphic detail about the storming of Drogheda and how Cromwell's soldiers slaughtered the entire garrison. We were told that a group of men, women and children who took refuge in a church were burned alive when the church was deliberately torched.

Our historian told how the British continued to take shiploads of grain out of Ireland when hundreds of thousands of people were dying of starvation during the famine and how Queen Victoria had sent £5 to help those in distress.

He told us about the soup kitchens and how families were denied help unless they gave up their Catholic religion. He spoke with great bitterness about those who 'sold their soul for the penny roll, the soup and the hairy bacon'.

This Brother came in through the classroom door spitting venom and continued to do so throughout the lesson. His primary goal appeared to be, not to teach us history, but to instil in us a deep hatred of all things British. It was so bad that we all thought he needed psychiatric help. Word of his unorthodox approach got out and the Brother Provincial had him transferred back whence he came. He had been with us for a few months.

Meanwhile, in Loughmacrory, relationships between the Catholic and Protestant communities remained good, as outlined above. Let me give you a couple more examples.

Sam's uncle Robert used to play the accordion for us when we organised a Céili in the local hall—and he played the Soldier's Song (the Irish national anthem) at the end because that was what those present wanted.

There was a large area of bogland close to where we lived, and it was not unusual to see cows grazing there when they managed to escape from local fields. From time to time, a cow would get stuck in swampy land in the middle of the bog. As soon as the alarm went off, all available men rushed to the scene to get the cow out. No one stopped to ask who owned the cow.

My father loved playing the bagpipes, but the only way he could join a band was to become a member of the AOH[6]. He wasn't interested in politics; he just wanted to play music. He often spoke of how they cooperated with a Protestant band in Sixmilecross. The bands would never be marching at the same time or attending the same events. This meant that if either band was short of instruments, banner poles, or whatever, they could borrow from the other. This was a frequent occurrence and worked to the mutual benefit of both bands.

I was not aware of any animosity between the AOH and the Orange Order. I was aware of a deep division within the Catholic Community in Loughmacrory. This was not always obvious, but at election time, the chasm became very wide. Sometimes families whom I thought were good friends and neighbours wouldn't talk to one another and occasionally there would be fisticuffs. It took me some time to work out what the problem was. The AOH was pro-Treaty, i.e., they supported the Anglo-Irish Treaty signed by Michael Collins in 1921 which ended the Irish War of Independence. They accepted the partitioning of Ireland. A bitter civil war broke out between the pro- and anti-treaty groups. The anti-treaty forces lost.

The civil war split, not just districts and communities, but families throughout Ireland. Loughmacrory was no different. The wounds were deep and slow to heal. I had come to realise

---

[6] The Ancient Order of Hibernians (AOH) was founded in New York City in 1836 to assist Irish Catholic immigrants, especially those who faced discrimination. It emerged in Ulster at the end of the nineteenth century with the aim of promoting Irish culture and traditions.

that I would be asked to kill for Ireland. Was it possible that volunteers could be asked to kill members of their own families? I had made my mind up. I wasn't going to die for Ireland. I was going to live for Ireland.

Chapter 3
Living for Ireland

When I decided that I was going to live for Ireland, I had in mind that I would do what I could to promote Irish music, Irish dancing, Irish sports, and the Irish language. But where to start?

Music was part of my growing up. My father played the bagpipes in a local band. He also played the violin. My eldest brother Joseph took an interest in the violin and became quite good at it. We had an old single-row, button key accordion which myself, my brother Paddy and sister Mary all learned to play.

In 1953, a group of us young people in the area decided to form a band. Paddy, Mary and I, our cousin Peter and a few others could already play the accordion, so we opted for an accordion band. I contacted a teacher from Pomeroy to train the accordion players while one of the local men trained the drummers. Training sessions were held mainly in Lenties' Hall.

We decided that we wanted to be an 'independent' band, rather than be part of any political party or grouping. It was very much a group of friends and neighbours from the Loughmacrory district—one family had five members; we had three, together with lots of our cousins. We enjoyed our time together as we were all a close-knit group who had grown up together and had known one another for many years. We enjoyed just being together as much as playing and marching.

There was widespread support for the band, and we were up and marching 'in no time'. We marched on all the religious feast days—St Patrick's Day, Easter, and August 15, as well as at local sports days and the like.

My uncle Jimmy was the eldest member of the band. He played the big drum. He had the furthest to travel as he lived in Mullaslin. This wasn't a problem as he had a motorbike. He was a bit of a character. I remember once he was telling my father how he had been at Carmen (Carrickmore) Fair and had got a great bargain in dinner plates. He bought six. On his way home, he skidded and fell off the bike. He wasn't injured and the bike wasn't damaged, but all the plates got broken. He couldn't get over the great bargain he had got in the plates— such good quality, and so cheap. He was sorry he hadn't bought a dozen!

I must have been born a teacher. I always felt the urge to share my skills and expertise with others. My time was heavily committed. Nonetheless, I did some football coaching, and I spent some time in the handball alley, encouraging the younger boys to strike the ball correctly using an underhand stroke and an open palm and to learn to use both hands.

Brother Nagel in Omagh CBS had instilled in me a great love of the Irish language and Irish culture. I decided to set up a branch of the Gaelic League. None of the people in Loughmacrory wanted to be involved at that time, but I found some kindred spirits in Mullaslin. We set up a branch based in Nugent's Hall. The governing body of the Gaelic League gave us a lot of independence. We were able to award scholarships to allow young people to go and study Irish in the Donegal Gaeltacht. I started organising Irish language and Irish dancing classes. I was happy enough to teach Irish language classes and Céili dancing classes myself but had never had an opportunity to learn step dancing. So, I engaged two dance teachers from Coalisland to do that.

I had taken on the role of raising money to buy accordions, drum kits and a uniform for the band, to pay the instructors, the dance teachers, and all other expenses. I got involved in organising céilis and dances. At first, I used Loughmacrory church hall. It was used mainly for church fundraising events, particularly around Christmas time, events like Tombola or whist drives. Father Dugan agreed that I could use it for my fundraising events. One of my first efforts was to invite Brian Caul and Frankie McBride—two of the rising stars in the various projects organised by Father Shields in Omagh—to sing in Loughmacrory. I remember paying their taxi fare from Omagh and giving them £5 each for their efforts. Both these men were to later form their own showbands and become famous on both the national and international singing circuits.

The hall in Loughmacrory was so small that it was difficult to raise enough money to cover expenses. So, I decided to move to Tracey's Hall in Mullaslin. Tracey's hall was not too expensive to hire, and I was able to make use of local bands. I did Master of Ceremonies (MC) myself to save money. And I did not engage a singer. Instead, during the interval, when the band was having a tea break, I used to sing.

My efforts were well received, and it became the norm that I would sing three songs during the interval.

A problem which I thought I had was that those attending wanted basic ballroom dances, more commonly referred to as 'English' dances. The most popular were the waltz, the foxtrot, and the quickstep. I wanted to introduce some Irish dances—I chose 'The Waves of Tory', 'The Walls of Limerick' and 'The Siege of Ennis' because they all involved multiple couples, were easy to learn and were good fun. The crowd agreed. Céili dancing became a compulsory part of the night's entertainment from then on.

Alcohol was sometimes a problem and on occasion, led to fights. When the group from Mountfield who disrupted the dance in Uncle Peter Ned's turned up, as they frequently did, they were usually under the influence and spoiling for a fight.

I found myself on many occasions trying to separate warring factions. I was never quite sure why they listened to me. Most of the protagonists were towering over me and could easily have pushed me to one side. However, I generally managed to restore peace. Perhaps my quiet, soft-spoken approach and refusal to take sides had a calming effect. In any event, I don't recall the fighting ever getting totally out of hand or resulting in serious injuries.

The crowds were getting bigger as our reputation for organising good events grew. I decided to move up the road to Nugent's Hall. It was bigger, always better organised with adequate stewards, so that drunks, and consequently fights, were less of a problem. Jim Daly's Céili Band from Coalisland was becoming well known throughout Tyrone and further afield. I invited Jim to Mullaslin. The crowd loved his music. This became our regular band.

I decided it was time to give the crowd a break from my singing efforts. I invited a little-known singer from Coalisland called Maisie McNally to come along with Jim. She was an instant hit. We had her back as often as she was available. Unfortunately for us, her fame was spreading rapidly and there was always a heavy demand for her time. She was later to become better known, both nationally and internationally, under her married name—Eileen Donaghy. Her husband was Tyrone footballer, Pat Donaghy (Their son Plunkett would later carry on the family footballing tradition).

Sometimes Maisie's sister Sally would come in her place and once her niece came. Her niece was still only a child when she came first but she had a voice like an angel. She, too, was an instant hit. She was later to become a well-known recording star, both in her own right and together with her husband as Ann and Francie Brolly.

Things took an unexpected turn when the IRA launched a campaign to create a United Ireland in 1956/57. However, this did not disrupt life to any great extent. I was able to continue in my role as promoter, MC, and occasional singer, and keep up with my studies, until the end of August 1957, when I completed my A-levels. I wasn't sure what I would be doing thereafter. It all depended on what results I got in my exams. But whatever lay in store for me, my love for Loughmacrory and its people would live on.

Chapter 4
The IRA Campaign 1956-57

The IRA Campaign 1956–57 was a campaign of urban guerrilla warfare carried out by the IRA against targets in Northern Ireland with the aim of overthrowing British rule and creating a United Ireland. This was the first major military undertaking since the 1940s when the harsh security measures of both the Irish and Northern Irish governments had severely weakened the IRA. In principle, the IRA wished to overthrow both the government in Belfast and the government in Dublin. In their eyes, both 'partitionist' states were illegitimate entities, imposed by Britain at the time of the Anglo-Irish Treaty in 1922. In practice, the IRA was, in the 1950s, focussing entirely on Northern Ireland.

By the mid-1950s, the IRA had substantially re-armed. This was achieved by means of arms raids, launched between 1951 and 1954, on British military bases in Northern Ireland and England. Arms were taken from Armagh, Derry, Omagh, Berkshire and Essex. In one raid alone—the raid on Gough Barracks in Armagh in June 1954—the IRA got away with a lorry-load of arms. An army audit revealed later that the IRA seized 250 Lee Enfield rifles, 37 submachine guns, 9 Bren guns and 40 training rifles.

It was hard to believe that the IRA was able to enter Gough Barracks, load a lorry with guns from the armoury and drive out unopposed. A similar operation in Omagh was less successful, but the raiders were still able to get clean away with a quantity of arms.

The IRA chose to launch their campaign in 1956 because they were encouraged by the results of the UK general election of 1955 when Sinn Féin candidates were elected MPs for the Mid-Ulster and Fermanagh and South Tyrone constituencies in Northern Ireland, with a total of 152,310 votes. This appeared to show that there was a substantial Irish republican support base within Northern Ireland. However, the IRA failed to consider the fact that the mainstream Nationalist Party had decided not to take part in the election. Consequently, its supporters had voted for Sinn Féin instead.

The 1956/57 campaign was a disaster for the IRA. Much to their consternation, they now discovered that they enjoyed practically no support from the nationalist population of Northern Ireland. A United Ireland was not a priority for the Nationalist community at that time. They wanted someone to address the social and economic issues faced by ordinary people. These issues were taken up by the Civil Rights Movement a few years later.

While it was a disaster for the IRA, it was a boon to the B-Specials. This group of Protestant men had been going through a lean time as there was very little for the part-time force to do. Now they found that their services were required almost on a full-time basis—a welcome opportunity to replenish dwindling resources.

The B-Specials were seen by Catholics as a bigoted, sectarian force and their behaviour during this period of IRA activity did little to dispel that view. Generally, they were deployed within their home area, so we had the situation where young men in police uniforms, armed with rifles, were stopping neighbours whom they had known all their lives and demanding to know their names, addresses, date of birth and proof of identity. This often led to conflict with heated words exchanged and young Catholics refusing to reveal their identity to their next-door neighbour who knew very well who they were. On occasion, fights broke out which sometimes ended up in court. I remember one judge ruling that the questioning was unreasonable since the parties involved had grown up together, had attended the same school and lived a few hundred yards apart. He dismissed the case. Unfortunately, common sense was sadly lacking in many of the judiciary at that time and the outcome was more likely to be a fine or a short prison sentence. All this achieved was a hardening of attitudes between Catholics and their Protestant neighbours.

Carrickmore was at that time, and probably still is, 99.9% Catholic. A group of Protestants from Sixmilecross decided to organise an Orange parade through it nonetheless. They knew there was no chance they would get away with it in normal circumstances, but they had a plan. They hired two buses—sufficient to transport the band and a group of supporters. They met in Sixmilecross at about 1 am. It was only a short drive to Carrickmore where they planned to arrive at 1.30 am when all inhabitants would be sound asleep. They would assemble at the foot of the town, the band would strike up with some Orange tunes, they would parade up the main street, remount the buses and be gone before the locals would have time to get dressed and launch any meaningful opposition.

There wasn't a sinner in sight when they arrived in Carrickmore. The plan seemed to have worked to perfection. They lined up behind the band, someone gave the order to march, the drums rolled, and the parade started up the street belting the music out at full blast.

No one anticipated that there was a major flaw in their strategy. They hadn't realised that pub-closing time in Carrickmore was flexible. The parade hadn't advanced far up the main street when the pub doors burst open, and hundreds of men rushed out and attacked the Orangemen. The invaders beat a hasty retreat, boarded their buses, and headed for home leaving much of their smashed-up equipment behind. They were not likely to come calling on my dad's band for the loan of equipment for their next outing!

Incidents such as the 'invasion' of Carrickmore were symptomatic of the strained relationships between the two communities. I tried not to let that influence my behaviour. I took my usual calm, pragmatic approach when stopped, answering questions as if I had never seen this man in uniform before. But I couldn't resist taking a hand out of[7] the B-Specials if the opportunity arose.

One night I was cycling home from Uncle John's, carrying a can of buttermilk, when I was stopped at a roadblock. At this stage, my bike was upmarket—fitted with a dynamo. After the usual questions, one of the Specials asked me if my lights were working. I said I thought they were. He asked me to show him. I said I couldn't do that. He asked why

---

[7] Making a joke at their expense.

and I said I couldn't manage to hold the buttermilk, lift the front of the bike, and spin the wheel to get the dynamo working. I suggested that one of the Specials hold the buttermilk, I would lift the bike, and a second Special could spin the wheel and check on the front light. It was working. Then they asked me if my rear light was working. I said I didn't know, as I couldn't see it when I was lifting the bike. So, we repeated the procedure but this time, the man who spun the wheel ran around to the back to check the rear light. I thanked them for their assistance. All was in order, so they let me go. They were probably feeling sorry for me since I couldn't manage to do anything without their help.

On another occasion, I was stopped close to the same spot, but this time the Specials were accompanied by a full-time member of the RUC. The police officer demanded to see my driving licence. He looked closely at it and then said, "You weren't wearing glasses when that photograph was taken."

I replied, "That's very observant of you. I can tell why you wanted to become a police officer." He scowled at me, and I thought for a moment I had overstepped the mark. Then he waved me on.

My Aunt Alice had come to live in Omagh at this stage and one day after school, I called down to see her. As I left her house on the Dromore Road to walk back to the bus station, I noticed that a deep hole had been dug on the opposite side of the road. I went over to see if there was any indication as to what was being constructed there. As I approached, two B-Specials stepped out with rifles at the ready to block my path. I said I just wanted to see whether this was a new building site. They told me that I was not allowed to get any closer. I asked them if they were afraid that I would fill the hole in. Their response was that I had better leave. I later learned that this was to be the site of the new telephone exchange.

In 1957, the IRA called a halt to their campaign. Even they accepted that it had been a disaster. This came as a bit of a shock to the B-Specials. They had been milking the system for all it was worth. A 24-hour guard on a hole in the ground was a good example. Their services would no longer be required. It was not good news for them.

Then one morning, we woke up to hear that a bomb had exploded under a bridge beside the Tyrone and Fermanagh Hospital—about two miles outside Omagh on the road to Carrickmore. The good news was that very little damage had been done and the road remained open. The good news for the B-Specials was that the order to stand down was rescinded.

The proverbial dogs in the street knew that the B-Specials had planted the bomb themselves. But this did not prevent the police from looking for a scapegoat. They decided to arrest my brother Eddie. Eddie was home on leave from the Irish army where he was based with the engineers. The police insisted that this meant he had knowledge of explosives and consequently, he was the number one suspect for planting the bomb. He was remanded in custody to Crumlin Road Prison in September 1957.

Eddie was held in Crumlin Road for four months without a single court appearance. The police didn't have a shred of evidence against him. The fact that he was in the Irish army would not be accepted in court as evidence that he had planted a bomb outside Omagh. The police had taken away all our books on the struggle for Irish independence. These could not be presented as proof of anything either. Eventually, Eddie was released without charge, and without apology. The police promised to return all the books they had taken away. They never did.

Chapter 5
At Crossroads

It was difficult to know what path to follow for a future career. There wasn't really a wide choice of professions for young Catholics in those days since Catholics had few opportunities for advancement in most professions. I saw my choice as being restricted to becoming a priest, a teacher, or a doctor. I considered a few other professions. Life as a commando appealed to me, but I ruled that out because there was no way I wanted to be involved in the slaughter of fellow human beings. Meteorology was something which interested me greatly, as was Forestry. But both would have meant going to England to study. I was put off by the thought of conscription. All male British subjects between 18 and 51 years old, as well as all females between 20 and 30 years resident in Britain, were liable to be called up for military service. Conscription did not apply to Northern Ireland. I was back to my three options. I decided to go for teaching.

I opted to do A-levels in Irish, Geography and Maths. In those days, only a minority of pupils took A-levels and the majority of those who did opted for two subjects. Some took three, but this was not the norm. I am amazed today to read of students taking five or more A-levels and gaining top marks in all of them. I am not convinced that it marks the evolution of super-geniuses.

I had not decided at that time whether I should go to St Joseph's Teacher Training College or to Queen's University to take a degree in Irish followed by a Post-Graduate Certificate in Education (PGCE) which would give me a qualification to teach. It really depended on my results. When my results came out, I believed my grades were good enough for a university scholarship. I can't remember the exact number of points required, but it was something like 65 and above to merit being offered the university route. My points score came to about 71 so I was disappointed when offered a scholarship to St Joseph's, but not to Queen's. I decided to ask 'why?' I stated my case to the man in charge of handing out the scholarships in the Omagh Council Office. He listened to what I had to say and then asked if I knew how many university scholarships he had given out to the CBS that year. I said, "No," to which he replied, "13." He then asked whether I knew how many scholarships he had given out to the Protestant grammar school. Again, I said, "No," and he replied, "5." He then went on to say, "If you think I am going to give any more university scholarships to the CBS, you have another think coming. Count yourself lucky to be getting a scholarship to St Joseph's." These were not his exact words. I have left out words which appeared to be Anglo-Saxon in origin.

It was the first time I had encountered discrimination. This was something new to me but something of which I was becoming increasingly aware. My brother Eddie was attending the local Technical College, and his favourite subject was technical drawing. Short Brothers (Aerospace

Company) was recruiting for their drawing office and came to Omagh Technical College looking for young people with development potential. Students in my brother's class were offered the opportunity to sit a test with a view to selection. Eddie passed with flying colours, was told of his success, and told that a letter would be issued in the next week or so to advise him about a starting date. A couple of weeks later, he received a form which had to be completed and returned. One question on the form asked what primary school he had attended. The answer to that question was 'St Teresa's Primary School'—clearly a Catholic school. He heard nothing further about the job offer.

A friend, who was studying shorthand and typing at Omagh Tech, had a similar experience. She was top of her class and was advised that she had been selected to follow a teacher-training course which would allow her to teach those subjects in similar institutions. She, too, completed an application form which included a question on primary school attended. She returned the form but heard nothing further about the offer.

I was later to learn that this was common practice and an easy way to distinguish Catholic applicants from their Protestant counterparts. It is difficult to identify religious denominations from the applicant's name alone. Secondary school attended is not always reliable. For example, anyone attending the Christian Brothers' Grammar School is almost guaranteed to be a Catholic, but pupils attending 'The Tech' could be of either denomination. However, Catholic primary schools are almost invariably called after saints, Protestant primary schools are not.

Getting back to my own situation, I learned from my father the importance of meeting discrimination with dignity and discipline. The lessons he taught me were summed up eloquently by Martin Luther King on the steps of the Lincoln Memorial in Washington, DC some six years later (28 August 1963):

In the process of gaining our rightful place, we must not be guilty of wrongful deeds. Let us not seek to satisfy our thirst for justice by drinking from the cup of bitterness and hatred.

I was not aware of any way I could complain about the attitude of the man dispensing scholarships in Omagh Council Office, or appeal against his decision. Martin Luther King expressed my thoughts concisely in that exquisite address. There was no point in 'wallowing in the valley of despair'. I must move on and 'hew out of the mountain of despair a stone of hope'. I accepted the scholarship to St Joseph's (Trench House).

I started my course in Trench House in September 1957. The IRA ended its campaign earlier that year. But the police were still on high alert and sometimes did random stop and search. Let me tell you of a few encounters which I hope will make you smile.

Caught in Possession of Pondweed

I recall one night in October/November 1957, there was something on in the college. My cousin Peter, friend Dessie and I were walking up Andersonstown Road in West Belfast, on our way to Trench House, when we were stopped by the police. They identified us as potential terrorists as we walked along chatting and laughing. They stopped us and asked where we were going. They weren't fooled when we said, "Trench House," and asked us to empty our rucksacks so that they could see what we were carrying. Mostly the rucksacks contained books and sports gear, but I had one item which they identified immediately as a potential bomb.

I was involved in a project with our rural science lecturer. He had asked if any of us could bring in some pond life from a local pond so that we could discuss what we had found. When I emptied my rucksack, the police spotted a large jam jar full of strange dark liquid—a potential bomb if ever they had seen one. I told them what it was, but they wouldn't believe me. They looked at it carefully from every angle. It seemed clear to me that nature study had not featured in their education. They stood well back as I took the lid off the jar so that they could have a closer look. I invited them to put their finger in and check that it was just water with pondweed and water insects. The look on their face suggested that they were concerned that I might have a crocodile, conger eel or some other dangerous creature in there which would take their finger off. They asked me to replace the lid and waved us on our way. I think they were glad to get rid of us!

A Case of Road Rage

But the police weren't the only ones wanting to keep us on the straight and narrow. I was in my third year in Trench House and was a qualified basketball referee. I would generally get a lift to basketball matches with another friend, Seamus, who was also a referee. He drove a tiny little two-seater sports car and I was always amused when watching him lowering his huge frame into this tiny space. He was a super athlete. He played international basketball and international water polo for Ireland. He was British No 2 in the Decathlon and had competed in the Commonwealth Games.

I recall once we were on our way to a basketball match and Seamus wasn't 100% sure of the way. We had almost drawn level with a road where we had to turn left. Seamus was in the outside lane and quickly cut across to turn left up the Whiterock Road, in West Belfast. The driver behind didn't take kindly to Seamus cutting across and blasted his horn. Then he followed us up the Whiterock Road, roared past and swung in in front forcing Seamus to stop. He jumped out of his car and came to the driver's window, glowering down at Seamus. He was a big man, about 6' tall, with the appearance of a bodybuilder—muscles everywhere. He was wearing a sleeveless vest which showed off his bulging and heavily tattooed arms. He glowered at Seamus and said, "Get out of the…car." Seamus asked what the problem was. The driver replied, "You cut me off. Get out of the car." Seamus got out of the car and drew himself up to his full height. The other driver looked up at him—a good 5" taller with shoulders like the back of a bus. I have never seen road rage dissipate so quickly! He drew in his breath and said, "I just wanted to tell you that your indicators don't appear to be working."

The Case of the Missing Loaves

In March 1960, Northern Ireland had a bread strike and as the shortage of bread became an increasing concern the province's Minister of Labour and National Insurance, Mr

Ivan Neill, was forced to intervene to prevent the situation from deteriorating.

To cope with the extra demand for bread, bakers at Omagh Model Bakery were working extra shifts and their van men were also working overtime. Extra shifts were being worked by three other home bakeries in Omagh. There was no shortage of bread in Co Tyrone.

I was on teaching practice in Loughmacrory Primary School, about ten miles from Omagh. There was no shortage of bread for us. I decided to bring some bread up to the family I stayed with while attending Trench House. I managed to squeeze four loaves into a suitcase and took an early train to Belfast on a Saturday morning. I called up to my 'digs', gave my landlady the bread and then headed back downtown to wait for my dad who was coming home from Scotland where he was working at that time.

I was a little early, so I was wandering around Smithfield. I was just window-shopping as there were no shops open. I noticed two policemen watching me. They came over to me and asked me what I was doing. I said I was waiting for my dad. They asked what was in the case. I said, "Nothing." They wanted to know why I was carrying an empty case around. I said, "It wasn't empty when I left home." Of course, they wanted to know what had been in it. They were sceptical when I said, "Bread," pointing out that it wasn't possible to buy four loaves of bread anywhere in Belfast because of the strike. I explained that I had bought the bread in Loughmacrory.

That started another line of questioning. Where is Loughmacrory?—Co Tyrone. What is the nearest town?—Carrickmore. They had never heard of either. One officer was busy taking notes. He asked if my postal address was:

Loughmacrory, Carrickmore. I replied, "No, it is Loughmacrory, Omagh." He then thought he would get on firmer ground and asked me if I knew whether Loughmacrory was in the Carrickmore police division or Omagh police division. I replied, "Neither, it is in Mountfield police division."

He stopped writing and said, "This isn't making a lot of sense."

I replied, "You can't blame me for that. Common sense isn't all that common amongst local councillors in general. And no one asked me for advice."

At that point, I spotted my dad and waved to him to let him know where I was. I turned to the police officers and said, "If you have no more questions, we will head for the train and get back home to Loughmacrory." They said I was free to go. I guess they decided I had been telling the truth. No one could make up a story like that.

One Turn Too Many

Once I hired a car and was trying to find my way through central Belfast. I suddenly realised that I was going the wrong way on a one-way street. I was looking for a place to turn when a policeman flagged me down. He asked, "Did you not see the arrows?"

I was tempted to say, 'I didn't even see the Indians'. But I bit my tongue and said, "I am a bit lost. I didn't notice until I saw two cars coming towards me. I am looking for a place to turn." He asked for my name and address. The response was the same as that given to the police officers in Smithfield.

This officer had never heard of Loughmacrory, Carrickmore or Mountfield. He wasn't even sure where Omagh was.

He said, "You are a long way from home." He stopped the traffic to allow me to turn and warned me to be more careful next time.

I qualified as a teacher in 1961. I started my teaching career in Strabane, Co Tyrone, where John Hume was also teaching. I first met John at St Joseph's Training College. He had followed the route I had hoped to follow. He took a degree in Irish at Queen's University and then a PGCE at St Joseph's. We had much in common. I was looking forward to getting to know him better. However, I didn't stay long in Strabane. I was offered a senior post in a school in Downpatrick, Co Down—an offer I couldn't refuse. Two years later, I was on the move again. I was offered a Head of Department post at St Peter's Secondary School in West Belfast. I accepted the post. My colleagues in Downpatrick told me I was crazy leaving a quiet, country school where the boys were extremely well-behaved and moving to the city where they believed, the boys would 'eat me alive'.

Little did any of us know what lay ahead.

Chapter 6
St Peter's Secondary School and the Tripartite System of Streaming Children

St Peter's Secondary School was situated in Britton's Parade, Whiterock Road, West Belfast. (It later merged with Corpus Christi College). It was unusual in that it was situated in St John's parish in the Upper Falls but catered for boys from St Peter's parish in the Lower Falls area. St John's had its own secondary school, St Thomas's, a little bit further up the Whiterock Road. The Lower Falls, like all of West Belfast, was an economically deprived area with high unemployment, high-density, poor-quality housing and more than its share of dysfunctional families.

Several teachers in the new school had taught for years in a range of primary schools in St Peter's parish so they knew most of the boys well. Until St Peter's Secondary School opened in 1964, boys and girls in St Peter's parish, who failed the 11+ exam, or didn't sit the 11+, stayed on in their primary school until they were 14 or 15. The teachers who knew them warned us that pupils from the Lower Falls had a reputation for vandalism and bad behaviour. They told me that I would find a dramatic change from the well-behaved boys I had taught in Strabane and Downpatrick. If discipline was to be maintained, every teacher needed to arm him or herself with a heavy-duty strap. Corporal punishment was not only acceptable in those days—it was expected.

I had a different perspective on discipline than most teachers. The principal and most of the staff demanded respect and discipline was to be strictly enforced with the liberal use of the strap. I believed that I had to earn respect and that I could not expect the boys to respect me unless I respected them. I was not anticipating any discipline problems. Besides, I chose teaching as a career because I wanted to help under-achieving boys carve out a better future for themselves. With a catchment area like that discussed above, I would expect to find many under-achievers in the D-streams in St Peter's. This seems like a good time to explain what we mean by 'secondary modern schools' and 'streaming' for those who are not au fait with the terminology.

The idea of streaming children of presumed different intellectual abilities originated in England in the interwar period. Three levels of secondary school were planned:

1. Academic grammar schools for pupils deemed likely to go on to study at university.
2. Central/technical schools would provide artisan and trade training for boys and/or domestic skills, such as cookery, laundry and sewing, for girls.
3. Secondary modern schools would provide basic secondary education.

In practice, few central/technical schools were created, and those that were created merged with secondary modern schools. As a result, the planned tripartite system became a bipartite system in which children who passed the eleven-plus examination were sent to grammar schools and those who failed, or didn't sit the test, were sent to secondary modern schools. This bipartite system applied in England and Wales and in Northern Ireland.

The government claimed parity of esteem between schools. The practice made a mockery of this claim. Secondary modern schools were officially designated as the school for failures where those who had failed their 11+ would receive training in a wide range of <u>simple</u> but practical skills. The purpose of this education was to focus on training in basic subjects, such as arithmetic, mechanical skills such as woodworking or domestic skills, such as cookery.

An unintended consequence of streaming was that most children attending grammar schools came from middle-class families while most children attending secondary modern schools came from working-class families.

The government went on to add insult to injury. Grammar schools were funded at a higher per-student level than secondary modern schools. Secondary moderns were generally deprived of both resources and good teachers. Staff turnover was high and continuity in teaching was minimal. In short, secondary schools were neglected by the authorities.

The better funding of grammar schools meant that middle-class children experienced better-resourced schools offering superior future educational and vocational options, while working-class children experienced comparatively inferior schools offering more limited prospects for educational and vocational progress. This reinforced class divisions in subsequent vocational achievement and earning potential.

There were further complications. The 'baby boomer' generation was particularly affected in the years 1957 to 1970 because grammar school places had not been sufficiently increased to accommodate the large bulge in student numbers which entered secondary schools during this period. As a result, cut-off standards on the 11+ for entry into grammar schools rose and many students who would, in earlier years, have been streamed into grammar schools were instead sent to secondary modern schools.

Consequently, many students in secondary modern schools were labelled 'failed the 11+' when the real problem was that the government had failed to provide sufficient places in grammar schools for all those who had passed the test. These academically able students suffered a double whammy when they found that their potential progression to university and advanced post-secondary studies was constrained by limitations within the secondary schools, the wider educational system and access to higher external examinations.

St Peter's Secondary School had three principals during the ten years I was there. Let me comment briefly on the first principal. He was an outstanding academic and was brought in to launch the school. It was understood that he would retire once the Board of Management was satisfied that things had stabilised. He attempted to raise the status of the school by requiring all staff to wear academic gowns. A few of us had a word with him and he agreed to make the wearing of gowns optional. All the staff dispensed with their gowns, except for the principal and vice-principal.

I am critical of how the principals of the secondary schools in West Belfast handled the task they were given, but accept that they were dealt a near-impossible hand. What was needed was principals who believed that every child should be given the chance to be educated to the limit of his/her talents. Clearly, not every child has an equal talent or an equal ability or an equal motivation, but they all have an equal right to develop what talent they have, to make something of themselves. The role of the school should be to help them become the best they can be.

The principals decided to prove that secondary schools were not the 'schools for failures', as labelled by the government. I agreed with their decision, but not with how they went about it. The pupils were streamed A to D along similar lines to the original tripartite system.

'A' designated the grammar school stream, those pupils who were deemed to have the ability to study for O- and A-levels and possibly go on to university.

'B' designated those with the potential to do O- and, possibly, A-levels, but who were unlikely to get the top grades.

'C' denoted those who would be better off aiming for a trade.

If we consider that the top pupils were skimmed off by the 11+; the best of those who failed the 11+ were skimmed off for the A-stream, second-best for the B-stream, third best for the C-stream. The members of D-stream hadn't been selected for anything; they were just discarded. They are the jetsam[8] of the education system.

---

[8] Flotsam and jetsam are terms that describe two types of marine debris associated with vessels. Flotsam is defined as debris in the water that was not deliberately thrown overboard. It may have been

So why should these pupils even bother trying to learn? I don't think the principal or most of the staff realised the negative impact being stamped with a 'D' had on these pupils. No one should be surprised if they were disruptive in class or simply didn't bother turning up. Most of the teachers dreaded having to teach them.

I said above that my focus was on under-achieving boys and that these would be found in the D-streams.

The principals set out to prove that secondary modern schools were just as good as, if not better than grammar schools. They were probably better in that there were fewer pupils studying for O-levels and A-levels and so the pupils would get more personal attention.

While criticising the government for funding grammar schools at a higher per-student level than secondary modern schools, all our secondary modern schools were now giving priority to academic achievement. St Peter's was no exception.

In due course, the teachers were proud to point out that one boy qualified as a doctor of medicine and practised as a GP. Another boy qualified as a solicitor. Others became teachers, some gained high positions in the civil service. These boys all failed the 11+ but went on to do exceptionally well in their chosen careers. The school rightly took credit for these success stories. Who would blame them? The role of the teacher is to identify skills which the children already have

---

lost overboard as a result of stormy weather, an accident or a shipwreck. Jetsam describes debris that was deliberately thrown overboard because it was believed to be of no use to anyone. These items had been discarded.

and help them develop those skills to the maximum. St Peter's played a key role in helping those boys achieve their objectives.

Most teachers see their role as passing on their expert knowledge to the pupils who passively absorb it. This is John Dewey's image of education[9]—the pupils arrive like empty bottles on a conveyor belt. The teacher fills them up with knowledge as they pass through.

My philosophy of education is guided by that of Plato, Aristotle, and the ancient Greeks, and in the later teachings of St Augustine. The Greek philosophers saw education as the awakening of the dormant potential within the individual. Success should not be measured solely by the number of children achieving O-levels and A-levels, success should be measured by the extent to which the teachers help all children to be the best they can be.

To be fair to the teachers—John Dewey's approach needs little investment of oneself in the process. My approach requires a lot. To achieve maximum growth and witness the flowering of the full potential of the pupils, teachers must have a real respect for and understanding of the life experiences of the pupils.

It is not a child's IQ or social standing or economic background or religion, or colour or ethnicity that is important. It is their value as a person which is significant. Each child has a unique identity. We need to listen to, and value, each child.

---

[9] John Dewey was an American philosopher, psychologist, and educational reformer. He was one of the most prominent American scholars in the first half of the twentieth century.

My concern was that the school accepted no responsibility for those who fell by the wayside. Responsibility was considered to lie with the boys themselves—they were lazy or had a low IQ; or with their deprived home background or the environment they grew up in, which gave them no encouragement to do well at school. Teachers expected nothing from the boys who were stamped with a 'D' and, as a rule, that is what they got.

The teachers who knew these boys warned that the older boys in the D group were not really interested in education. They would frequently be disruptive in class. The only way to enforce discipline was through corporal punishment, hence the need for a heavy-duty leather strap. Some of the boys would pick their own leaving date and just stop coming. This was something to look forward to because these boys would most likely be the most disruptive ones. In their absence, the teachers could work with the boys who wanted to learn.

With warnings like this ringing in their ears, there was a notable shortage of volunteers when the principal was allocating teachers to these classes. There was a look of relief on his face when I advised him that I was willing to teach general subjects, as well as PE, to any of the D groups.

There was no focus in the school on getting these children to be the best they could be. My aim was to change that.

Chapter 7
We Need to Listen to, and Value, Each Child

In my experience, young people find it easier to talk about themselves when taking part in sporting activities than when placed in formal settings. This is where I decided to begin my efforts to convince the boys in the D-streams that all pupils in the school are of equal value, and that the teachers are willing to help them to make a success of their lives.

The pupils in the final year class in the D-stream were no more interested in PE than they were in general subjects. It was necessary to devise a challenging programme for them. I introduced them to a game of 'Pirates'[10]. The boys loved this game and were always exhausted leaving the gym. They wanted to play it all the time. But I had other challenges for them.

My friend Phil was head of the Irish department, but like me, he enjoyed working with the D-streams. He was an inter-

---

[10] For detailed information on 'Pirates' see p180 of *Big Boys Don't Cry*, An Autobiography by Dr Willie McCarney, published by Matador, 2015. Available as an ebook.

county Gaelic football star. Phil and I used to organise a football match once a week, between two teams picked from the older D-streams. This wasn't just a kick-around. It was a serious competition. Each game was a *Mars Bar Match*. A Mars bar in those days cost 7d. We asked each of the boys to chip in $3^1/_2$d. The winning team would get the Mars Bars. The boys played their hearts out. You would think their life depended on it. Every match was like a World Cup final.

Divis Mountain rises above West Belfast and the lower slopes are covered with houses. The ground rises steeply from St Peter's until it reaches *The Mountain Loney*, a narrow laneway (now long gone as the area is completely covered with houses) leading to the base of the mountain. Then the ground rose very steeply to the summit of the Black Mountain. I challenged the boys to come with me for a race to the top of the Black Mountain and back, about three miles. (The Black Mountain is the nearest summit and is not quite as high as Divis itself which stands further back). It was pretty-tough going! Many were exhausted by the time they got to the base of the mountain. The final climb to the summit was difficult—even at a walking pace. And they still had to make it back to the school—although that was all downhill.

So, we didn't take the 'racing' too seriously, at least in the early days. We would sit down halfway to the summit, and I would do a little teaching. I would point out where the school was and ask them to identify various landmarks in the city. Then I would ask them if they could locate the street where they lived. I would point to the blue haze over the city and talk about pollution. I would help them to identify the flora and fauna. I remember one of the boys telling me that he expected to see heather on the mountain—not realising that we were sitting in the heather. I would point out all the little streamlets and explain how they all come together to form the river Farset, which gave Belfast its name. The name of the city in Irish is 'Béal Feirste'. When that is translated into English, it means 'the mouth of the river Farset'. I would talk a bit about geology and explain how the caves were formed or history and explain how the caves were used at different times by pirates and highwaymen and by rebels during the rebellion in 1798. The boys enjoyed these impromptu lessons taken on the mountainside covering topics they wouldn't listen to in a classroom.

The boys in the academic streams were jealous and wanted to know what I could offer them. I said I could arrange for them to have Pirates during their PE lessons and I asked them if they would like me to organise a mountain race. I said I was sure the principal would agree to them having an afternoon off for the race itself and they could do the training in their own time. I suggested that we call it *The Three Peaks Marathon*. What I had in mind was closer to a half-marathon than a marathon, but it was a pretty-gruelling course. The first leg of the race from the school to the summit of the Black Mountain (at 1275 feet or 388m) would be the most difficult. The second leg would be from Black Mountain to Armstrong Hill. This would be a relatively flat leg, but as there were no roads in those days, it was over rather-rough terrain. The third leg was from Armstrong Hill to the summit of Divis (at 1562 feet or 476m). The climb was not so steep, but again, the terrain was pretty-rough. The final leg was a long one, but was downhill all the way from the summit of Divis, skirting round the Black Mountain and downhill to the school. I promised them that everyone would have the opportunity to go around the full course at least once before race day. The boys were as excited about the prospect of the race as I was.

I was amazed at how seriously the boys took the race. Some of these 'hard men' burst into tears when I refused them permission to continue beyond the first leg because they were clearly exhausted. They pleaded with me to be allowed to finish the race. They knew they had no chance of winning, but they wanted to complete the race, just for their own satisfaction. I explained the dangers to them and promised that we would try to let them have another go at the circuit before the end of the school year—on condition that they trained hard.

The race was so popular that it was one of the highlights of the school year and became an annual event. Some of the boys would keep up long-distance running and one would later win the Belfast marathon, setting a record in the process which stood for years.

Discipline was not a problem. The strap which I had bought was lying on the desk in my office. The boys were in and out of my office regularly as they had free access to come and talk to me. One day my strap disappeared. I told the boys that I had misplaced my strap and asked them to let me know if they came across it. It never turned up and I never replaced it.

In my view, corporal punishment doesn't solve anything. I had a good relationship with the boys. I called them by their first name. I said please and thank-you when I asked them to do something for me. In our many informal chats, I let them know that I was interested in them as individuals. Some of them said the 'D' word meant—'dunce'—and told me they were useless, fit only to be bin men or road sweepers. I explained what a critical role these two professions played in the life of the city. If teachers went on strike, city life would continue as normal. But if the bin men and road sweepers went on strike, the place would be in chaos in no time.

I told them that the most important thing was to be the best they could be—whatever job they ended up in. I said I was sure they knew professionals who were not good at their jobs and took no pride in their work. I urged them to keep in mind the philosophy that if a job is worth doing it is worth doing well, irrespective of what that job happens to be.

I discussed whatever I was planning to do with them and asked for their comments. The boys knew I liked and respected them. They respected me in return. Discipline wasn't a problem.

I asked them if they would like to be involved in a community service project. There were old people living close to the school who didn't seem to have any family to help them out. Each of the boys would 'adopt a granny' and offer what help he could. The boys liked the idea and agreed to participate.

All the grannies were very happy with the scheme. They liked getting little jobs done for them. But, most of all, they enjoyed the company. The boys were enjoying it too. They knew the grannies looked forward to them coming and that they had come to depend on them. Some of the boys had no experience of anyone depending on them before. Up until now, most of these boys found it well-nigh impossible to make it to school for a 9 o'clock start. Now here they were meeting me at the school gate at 8 am to take on their caring role.

I was concerned about the number of boys who left school almost entirely lacking in literacy and numeracy skills. I was convinced that even those with a low IQ could achieve more if more was expected from them. I decided to start night classes in St Peter's in September 1967. I was expecting that the clientele would be mainly male, but the classes were open to all comers, male or female. The students would be given an opportunity to improve their literacy and numeracy, and to develop skills in woodwork, metalwork, arts, and crafts that would help them find employment. The students had to be at least 16 to attend night classes so the majority would have left school. There was no upper age limit.

We would, of course, offer advanced classes in English and Maths where students could work towards O-level or improve their grades if they had already sat these exams but had not done as well as they expected. Students who had stayed on at school could attend so long as they were over 16.

Sporting activities were always very popular so there were classes in gymnastics, basketball, badminton, and 5-a-side soccer.

The literacy and numeracy classes were well attended because I had managed to identify two teachers who were experts in these areas and experienced in working with adults. Sometimes the students were reluctant to admit that they couldn't read or write. I would sit down with them and talk it over. I would point out that there was no need to feel ashamed. The only shame would be if they were to bypass the opportunity to do something about it. Most importantly, they would not be treated as if they were children at the beginning of their primary school career. The textbooks had been specially written for adults.

I recall two boys who told me that their biggest shame was in being stopped and questioned by the army. There were frequent allegations of abuse and some regiments had adopted the procedure of asking those who had been detained to sign a form to say they hadn't been abused. These boys had been arrested on several occasions because they refused to sign the form. They said they would rather be arrested than admit that they couldn't read or write. After a long chat with me, the boys agreed to 'give it a try'. As they left, one turned to me and said, "Right, back to *Dick and Dora*" (first reading books for Primaries 1 and 2).

There were nearly as many students enrolled at night as there were during the day. Most of the staff taught full-time in St Peter's but were happy to earn a bit extra in the evenings. They knew all the students who were past pupils of the school, and the boys knew them. So, everything went smoothly. The good behaviour of the former St Peter's boys set a good example for the others.

I recall two boys who came in wishing to register for classes. Everyone had to fill-in a form and one of the questions asked, 'School attended?' I didn't recognise these two boys and knew they had never been to St Peter's. I overheard one of the boys whispering to the other, "How do you spell St Thomas's?"

The second boy responded, "How the…would I know. Put down 'St Peter's', like I did."

At this time also, discussions were taking place in the BELB[11] about the possibility of launching a summer scheme which would run for about six weeks. I was asked if I would

---

[11] Belfast Education and Library Board.

develop a pilot programme in St Peter's. Unlike the night classes, the scheme would cater for boys and girls of school age.

Some of you may wonder how I managed to achieve so much autonomy that I could make such decisions without consulting anyone. I can only say that the first principal did not intend to be around very long. Perhaps he saw me as a contender to take over his role. I had no intention of applying but I had lots of ideas of things I wanted to do. I was happy to be free to get on with it. The second principal had his own selfish reasons for letting me try things out. But I didn't know that until later.

I worked very closely with the PE[12] Advisor to the BELB. He agreed to provide me with whatever additional sporting equipment I needed. He provided two trampolines. He arranged to have McCrory Park, where we played Gaelic football, turned into an all-weather pitch, and provided with an additional set of goal posts so that we could use it for matches even if it rained during the summer.

I organised competitions in Gaelic football, hurling, soccer and basketball and got local businesses to sponsor trophies. There was so much demand from young people wanting to 'have a go' on the trampolines that we had to give them time slots. Gymnastics, too, was popular and we provided coaching in vaulting and mat work. Teachers in the woodwork and metalwork departments agreed to come in and assist young people in making things of their own choosing. The art teacher offered classes in pottery making. For those who were not interested in physical activity or in the various

---

[12] Physical Education.

classes offered, we provided quiet rooms where they could play board games or listen to music.

One of the local charities asked whether the boys who had been doing the community service would be willing to help-out, as part of the summer scheme, with delivering furniture to needy families. Several boys agreed and the charity loaned us their van. The boys were happy to be involved, as they knew many Catholic families in need. They were amazed on one occasion when I said we had a delivery to make to the (Protestant) Shankill Road. Why were we going there? Protestants were not in need. Protestants all had good jobs, plenty of money, nice houses—not at all like the families in Catholic West Belfast. None of the boys had ever been in the home of a family in Protestant West Belfast before. They admitted on the way back that they would not have been able to tell the difference between a Protestant granny and a Catholic granny. This gave me an opportunity to explain once again that Catholics and Protestants had more in common than the things which separated them.

Unfortunately, this was not a good time to test my theory with our Protestant neighbours on the Shankill Road as the Rev Ian Paisley denounced Prime Minister Terence O'Neill's efforts to address Northern Ireland's simmering social and political issues as 'pandering to Catholics'.

Chapter 8
The Abominable 'No!' Man

From the creation of Northern Ireland in 1921, the Roman Catholic minority community suffered discrimination under the Unionist and wholly Protestant governments. The Catholic minority was politically marginalised. This was largely a product of Northern Ireland having been deliberately set up with an inbuilt two-thirds Protestant majority. It was exacerbated by the drawing of local government electoral boundaries to favour Unionist candidates, even in predominantly Catholic areas.

The practice of manipulating local government electoral boundaries was known as gerrymandering and was most blatant in Derry City, which had a clear nationalist majority. 8,800 Protestant voters returned 12 Unionist councillors, while 14,500 Catholic voters elected eight Nationalist councillors. A Catholic vote carried less than half the value of a Protestant vote in Derry!

The right to vote in local government elections was restricted to property owners—favouring Protestants—with those holding or renting properties in more than one ward receiving more than one vote, up to a maximum of six. Business owners, most of whom were Protestant, were also entitled to multiple votes. By controlling local government, Unionists were able to ensure that Protestant areas received more government investment than their Catholic neighbours.

The Rev Paisley had been active on the Northern Ireland political scene since 1950 and had been whipping up sectarian hatred for years. He was among those invited in 1956 to a special meeting at the Ulster Unionist Party's offices in Glengall Street, Belfast. The meeting's declared purpose was to organise the defence of Protestant areas against anticipated IRA activity. The new body called itself *Ulster Protestant Action* (UPA) and the first year of its existence was taken up with the discussion of vigilante patrols, street barricades, and drawing up lists of IRA suspects in both Belfast and rural areas.

On 17 June 1959, at a Belfast rally, the Rev Paisley publicly chastised the men of the Shankill for allowing 'papists, pope's men, and papishers' to live on the Shankill Road. Angry crowds went to the addresses called out by the Rev Paisley, burned out the occupants and looted their homes.

In 1964, he demanded that the Royal Ulster Constabulary[13] (RUC) remove an Irish tricolour from Billy McMillan's office in Divis Street, Belfast. McMillan was standing as a Republican candidate for the Belfast West constituency in the Westminster election. The public display of the flag of the Republic of Ireland was banned by the Northern Ireland government at that time. The Rev Paisley insisted that the RUC remove the flag, or he would organise a march and remove it himself. The police, fearing a backlash

---

[13] The official name of the Northern Ireland police force at that time. They were generally known as the RUC.

from loyalists, removed it. This led to two days of rioting in West Belfast.

Terence O'Neill replaced Lord Brookeborough as Prime Minister in 1963 and immediately introduced a variety of bold measures to improve the economy. At the same time, he realised that, for his programme of modernisation to succeed, he would also have to address Northern Ireland's simmering social and political issues. In a series of radical moves, he met with the Prime Minister of the Republic of Ireland (the Taoiseach), Seán Lemass—the first such meeting between Irish heads of government for 40 years. He also put out feelers to the nationalist community in the north.

The Unionist majority interpreted these initiatives as a serious threat since the Republic's constitution still laid claim to the whole island of Ireland. O'Neill's policies provoked outspoken attacks from within Unionism. The most vocal opposition came from the Rev Ian Paisley.

The Rev Paisley was actively whipping up Unionist fears regarding Terence O'Neill's initiatives. He co-founded the Ulster Constitution Defence Committee, and the Ulster Protestant Volunteers, a paramilitary organisation, on 17 April 1966 at a parade in the Shankill area of Belfast. The situation quickly reached a boiling point. Rioting and disorder erupted, culminating in the murder of two Catholics and a Protestant by a loyalist terror group called the Ulster Volunteer Force. These were the first victims in the cycle of sectarian bloodletting that would become known, post-1969, as *The Troubles.*

A journalist friend of mine (James/Jim Kelly[14]) who reported from Stormont from its inception for over 70 years, called Ian Paisley 'The Abominable 'No!' Man' because his response to any talk of reform was always: 'No! No! No!'

---

[14] Jim wrote his final column for the *Irish News* a couple of weeks before his 100th birthday. He died a few days before his final column was published.

Chapter 9
The Civil Rights Campaign—
Caledon 1968

The IRA misread the mood of the Catholic community when they launched their campaign in 1956. A United Ireland was not a priority for the Nationalist community at that time. They wanted someone to address discriminatory housing policies, discrimination in employment, and a fair drawing of electoral boundaries. They were impatient with the pace of reform and were unconvinced about Terence O'Neill's sincerity.

Discrimination over housing allocation had long been a source of anger for nationalists. Decisions were made by local councils, which tended to be Unionist-dominated. The right to vote was linked to property ownership, so refusing to allocate houses to Catholic families limited their right to vote and helped, along with gerrymandering, to perpetuate Unionist electoral dominance.

No one expected that Caledon, a small village in Co Tyrone, which few people have even heard of, would ignite Northern Ireland's Civil Rights Movement.

In 1968, the people of Caledon decided to make a stand against the Unionist-dominated Dungannon council. Their aim was to abolish the discriminatory housing policies practised by the council.

An informal agreement had been reached between a local priest and a Unionist politician that 15 houses built by the council would be allocated to an equal number of Protestant and Catholic families. However, the council decided that just one of these houses would be allocated to a Catholic family, while the other 14 homes would be allocated to Protestant families.

One of the homeless Catholic families decided to squat in an empty house. After eight months in the house, they were charged with squatting. The judge ruled that they could stay in the house for up to six months to allow the council time to review its decision. Six months later in June 1968, the RUC smashed the door down and dragged the family out—watched by supporters and the media.

It then became known that a 19-year-old single girl had been allocated the house next door. She was a Protestant and secretary to a Unionist politician. Another homeless Catholic family decided to squat in this house, together with Austin Currie MP. A couple of hours later, they were ejected from the house and subsequently charged with breaking and entering the house and squatting.

All hell broke loose. Austin Currie made a claim of blatant discrimination and took the case through all the proper channels but achieved nothing. In Stormont, John Taylor MP strongly defended the actions of the council and during a stormy session, Austin Currie was ordered by the speaker to leave the Assembly Chamber. In protest, Currie went back to the council house in Caledon and occupied it with two friends until they were evicted by police. Currie had alerted the media. Images were flashed round the world. A campaign for the fair allocation of housing, led by Conn and Patricia McCluskey, had been under way in the Dungannon area since 1963. They founded the Campaign for Social Justice. However, the break-in and squat by Austin Currie MP, Patsy Gildernew and Joe Campbell in Caledon was the major catalyst which launched the Civil Rights Movement in Northern Ireland. The organisation was created to campaign for social justice on a range of issues including discrimination against Catholics in employment and housing and the gerrymandering of electoral boundaries. Inspired by the American civil rights movement, meetings were taking place between the Northern Ireland Civil Rights Association (NICRA), Republicans, and local councillors to discuss Austin Currie's proposal for a civil rights march.

Police harassment, exclusion from public service appointments and other forms of discrimination were factors of daily life in Tyrone, and throughout Northern Ireland, while I was growing up. Despite my personal experiences, I was not drawn to join the NICRA. I was aware that, following the disastrous campaign in 1956–57, the IRA had moved to the left to regain community support. The civil rights campaign had strong community support and Sinn Féin wanted to be part of it. Sinn Féin was banned in 1956, but reorganised under the name of 'Republican Clubs' or, simply, 'Republicans'. They threw themselves behind the NICRA, swelling the number of active members. Some got involved in the leadership. I believe that the NICRA should be non-sectarian, and non-violent. I was not convinced that Republican Club members were on the same wavelength.

On 24 August 1968, NICRA organised a protest march from Coalisland to Dungannon. The march was publicised as a 'civil rights march', and the organisers emphasised its non-sectarian dimension. The police stopped the march from entering Dungannon, where a counter-demonstration had been called by the Rev Paisley's supporters. NICRA organisers announced that they would not breach the police cordon. The marchers sat down and blocked the road.

A second civil rights march was organised by the Derry Housing Action Committee (DHAC) on 5 October 1968. The march was banned by the Minister for Home Affairs, William Craig. The ban was ignored. The marchers were demanding an end to gerrymandering, an end to discrimination in housing and the right to vote. The RUC attempted to violently disperse the crowd and chaos erupted. Images of police brutality, including a photograph of Gerry Fitt MP with blood pouring from a wound in his head, caused by a police baton, were broadcast worldwide.

On 9 October, 2,000 students from Queens University organised a march to Belfast City Hall to protest against police brutality. The students formed a new organisation which they called *People's Democracy* (PD). It demanded more radical reforms of the government of Northern Ireland than NICRA. The key demands were: one man, one vote; a fair drawing of electoral boundaries; freedom of speech and assembly; repeal of the Special Powers Act[15]; and a fair

---

[15] The Civil Authorities (Special Powers) Act was passed by the Northern Ireland parliament in April 1922. The Special Powers Act gave the Northern Ireland government, and by extension its police and security forces, extensive powers to deal with threats and

allocation of jobs and social housing. 'One man, one vote' became the central demand of the movement.

On 22 November 1968, Terence O'Neill announced the dissolution of Derry Corporation, the end of multiple votes for company directors and a points system to end housing discrimination. O'Neill made a television address appealing to the Civil Rights Movement to 'give him time' to introduce reforms. NICRA and the DHAC responded by calling a truce.

In January 1969, the PD organised a 'Long March' from Belfast to Derry modelled on the civil rights march to Montgomery, Alabama. NICRA and DHAC opposed the march because they feared it would raise sectarian tension. The PD supporters insisted that it was merely an attempt to expose the dirt which had been swept under the carpet.

The march was attacked repeatedly along the way by various Protestant groups. The police made no effort to protect the marchers. The marchers were ambushed at Burntollet Bridge, outside Derry, by a large group of loyalists which included members of the RUC and the B-Specials. Eighty-seven marchers were hospitalised. When the marchers reached Derry, the city exploded in riots. Following a night of rioting, the RUC entered the Bogside (a Catholic ghetto), wrecked a number of houses and beat up residents, one of whom died. Another man died as a result of a police assault in Armagh.

------

disorder in the Six Counties. The Act also included severe punishments, such as flogging, and internment without trial for those arrested under its provisions. It was used mainly against Catholics and was seen by the Irish nationalist community as a tool of Ulster unionist oppression.

It was clear that O'Neill's days as Prime Minister were numbered as the Rev Ian Paisley had whipped up opposition to a fever pitch once more over his 'pandering to Catholics'. In March and April 1969, there were six bomb attacks on electricity and water infrastructure targets, causing blackouts and water shortages. At first, the attacks were blamed on the Irish Republican Army (IRA). It later emerged that members of the loyalist Ulster Protestant Volunteers (UPV) and the Ulster Volunteer Force (UVF) had carried out the bombings to implicate the IRA, destabilise the government and halt the reforms demanded by the Civil Rights Movement and promised by the Prime Minister. This proved to be the final nail in the coffin. O'Neill was forced to resign on April 28, 1969, and was replaced by James Chichester-Clark.

The Northern Ireland government introduced more-repressive legislation (specifically banning civil disobedience tactics such as sit-ins), which led to further protests across the North. At the same time, Chichester-Clark, under pressure from the British Prime Minister, Harold Wilson, announced the introduction of 'one man, one vote' promised by O'Neill, as this would bring Northern Ireland into line with the rest of the UK. But the Civil Rights campaigners now had additional demands concerning police violence and state repression. There were calls for the abolition of the Special Powers Act, which gave almost unlimited power to the state (including internment without trial) and the disbandment of the B-Specials.

Chapter 10
In the Eye of the Storm

On 12 August 1969, an Orange Order parade in Derry was allowed by the police to pass by the Catholic Bogside leading to an outbreak of rioting. The RUC attacked the residents, leading to *The Battle of the Bogside*, which lasted for three days (August 12–14, 1969). The NI government mobilised the B-Specials with a view to reclaiming control of the area.

While the first victims in the cycle of sectarian bloodletting were two Catholics and a Protestant murdered by the loyalist terror group, the Ulster Volunteer Force, in 1966, the events of August 1969 are widely regarded as the beginning of the thirty-year conflict known as *The Troubles*. Sporadic violence occurred across the North on a daily basis and here, I highlight only the more significant incidents—in particular, those incidents which impacted the pupils in St Peter's Secondary School.

In support of the Bogsiders, nationalists and Catholics launched protests elsewhere in Northern Ireland. The bloodiest rioting was in Belfast. On 14 and 15 August 1969, loyalist paramilitaries, accompanied by members of the B-Specials attacked Catholic residents in the St Peter's parish area of the Lower Falls. Seven people were killed and hundreds more wounded. Scores of houses and businesses were burnt-out, most of them owned by Catholics. Some 3,500 Catholic families were driven from their homes. The RUC was accused of helping the loyalists and of failing to protect Catholic areas. Events in Belfast had all the appearance of a pogrom against the minority Catholic and nationalist community.

Since St Peter's parish bore the brunt of the attacks, many families sought refuge in St Peter's Secondary School in Britton's Parade. Some of those families stayed only a short time before finding temporary accommodation with extended family in the Andersonstown area on the western fringes of the city, but many were still in residence when the school reopened in September.

I oversaw the summer school. Consequently, it was assumed that I would deal with the refugee problem. I decided that the only way to clear the rooms to allow teaching to commence was to turn the gym and assembly hall into dormitories. This freed up the classrooms but meant that all PE classes had to be taken outdoors. It was not a major inconvenience since, as is often the case in September, the weather was good. The pupils were quite happy to be participating in outdoor activities, so I had no concerns about that. I was concerned, however, about the trauma that the majority had experienced in mid-August and wondered what impact it would have on them in the longer term. Only time would tell.

Catholics felt betrayed by all sides when the Protestant pogroms were launched against them. The 'forces of law and order' were obviously on the side of the Protestants. They were not going to come to the assistance of Catholics. When the British army was brought in to restore order, they built a barrier to separate the two sides. At first, it was a barbed wire barrier. This was replaced by corrugated iron, and, later by a brick wall. This was the first of Belfast's defensive walls, more commonly called 'Peace Walls'. More than 100 were built. They were intended to be temporary, but more than fifty years later, most are still standing, and have all the appearance of permanency. They played, and still play such an important role that I will come back to them later.

Because they felt so exposed and so vulnerable at that time, Catholics welcomed the British troops into their areas, literally with open arms. The relationship between the British army and the Catholic population was initially very cordial, with women bringing cups of tea and sandwiches to the soldiers on guard duty.

Confrontations initially were between the army and Protestant paramilitaries. Three people were shot dead during street disturbances in the Shankill area of Belfast on 11 October 1969. Two were civilians shot by the British army and one was an RUC officer shot by suspected loyalists. He was the first RUC officer to die in *The Troubles.*

This was rather an anomalous situation—Catholics who, by and large, supported the idea of a United Ireland, being protected by the forces of the British Crown from those people who professed allegiance to that Crown and who regarded the British army as their army. This was not a situation which the Unionist government, based at Stormont, or the RUC, could tolerate, and a campaign began to direct the British army to where the 'real' enemy could be found.

Relationships with the Catholic community deteriorated quickly, and confrontations became more frequent when the army was misinformed by Stormont government ministers and the RUC that the bombing of the electricity and water infrastructure earlier in the year was the work of the IRA. Those bombings, too, had in fact been carried out by Protestant paramilitaries who had now become increasingly active. However, government ministers and the RUC convinced the army commanders that the 'real' enemy was the Catholic paramilitaries and that they should turn their attention to them.

As confrontations increased, it became apparent that Catholics could no longer depend on the army to protect them in the event of further loyalist attacks. The Provisional IRA assumed the lead role as a defender of the Catholic community. Civil disobedience and street politics became increasingly unstable. Many activists, mainly from the nationalist community, were imprisoned and the army announced it would shoot rioters.

Following an Orange Order parade on 31 March 1970, intense riots erupted on Springfield Road in West Belfast. Violence lasted for three days, and the British army used CS Gas for the first time in large quantities. 38 soldiers and dozens of civilians were injured.

On 27 June 1970, following the arrest of Bernadette Devlin, a civil rights leader and a Nationalist MP, intense riots erupted in Derry and Belfast. Loyalist paramilitaries made incursions into republican areas of Belfast. This led to a prolonged gun battle between republicans and loyalists during which seven people were killed.

An illegal curfew (later to be declared legal retrospectively by an Act of the British Parliament) was declared in a Catholic area of West Belfast, incorporating all of St Peter's parish, from 3 to 5 July 1970, to enable the British army to carry out a search for guns. People were told they would be shot dead if they left their homes—three men were shot dead, while a fourth, an invalided ex-service man, was run over, spectators said deliberately, by an army Saracen[16]. But it was not the murders which upset people most.

For several days, no one was allowed to leave their homes to go to work or to purchase food or milk, even for young babies or those who were ill. Houses were extensively damaged during the searches and property was destroyed or looted. Religious pictures and statues were deliberately destroyed (the people were Catholic; the soldiers were, by and large, Protestant). Catholics had regarded the soldiers as their only defence against Protestant attacks. Now the soldiers had turned against them also. The Falls Road curfew was followed, in August 1971, by 'Internment'—Catholic men were rounded up and interned without trial on suspicion that they were in the IRA. The majority of those rounded up had no connections with the IRA and the bitterness and resentment against the British was now reaching boiling point.

In their desperation, people felt that their only hope was the IRA. But the IRA had been inactive for many years, apart from a brief campaign in 1956/57, and was completely disorganised. The total strength of the IRA in the area under curfew at that time is believed to have been in single figures with an 'arsenal' consisting of one 303 rifle, one Sten gun, which was not in working order, and a few revolvers. Some

---

[16] A Saracen is a six-wheeled armoured personnel carrier.

young men in the local communities vowed to set up their own defence force and call themselves the 'Provisional' IRA. Their intention was to hold the fort until the 'Official' IRA could be re-grouped and re-armed. It is ironic to think that the Northern Ireland government, intent on destroying the IRA, was its most effective recruiting agent. Hundreds of young men were queuing up to join. The Falls Road curfew and internment had a major impact on the formation of the Provisional IRA and on the campaign of terror and destruction which was to last for the next 30+ years.

During the operation, the soldiers came under attack from the IRA and Republican rioters. Five civilians were killed, sixty were injured and three hundred were arrested. Fifteen soldiers were injured.

Photographs released by the army and the RUC suggested that arms were being found by the lorry-load. However, keen-eyed observers noted that a Gatling gun featured prominently in almost every photograph. The Gatling gun is one of the best-known early rapid-fire weapons and a forerunner of the modern machine gun. It was first used in the American civil war in the 1860s. All models of Gatling guns were declared obsolete by the US army in 1911! So where had all these Gatling guns come from? Perhaps there was only one pile of arms which was simply rearranged to give the impression of many. Later research would confirm this view. Arms were uncovered in only 5% of the houses searched, much fewer than had been anticipated. The searches were so violent that the net effect was to increase support for the IRA and speed up recruitment.

Chapter 11
Dicing with Death

I faced many challenges in the summer scheme throughout this period but managed at all times to keep the ball rolling and maintain control. One such challenge was being faced with a group of young men in their 20s who wanted to participate. Under the rules, those wishing to join had to be under 20. But here I was faced with a rough bunch of lads who could cause no end of trouble if they put their minds to it. As I looked at their leader, John, I thought of the words of Lyndon B Johnson (36th President of the US): *I'd rather have him inside the tent pissing out than outside the tent pissing in.* John was no Edgar Hoover (Director of the FBI, and target of Johnson's comment) but I thought the President's words were very appropriate in the current context.

I explained the rules to John and his gang and said there wasn't a lot I could offer them. However, I was prepared to let them participate in the senior outdoor five-a-side soccer competition. They would have to stick to the rules like everyone else and I would have the final decision in any dispute. John said they were happy with that and then asked if they could have a room for darts if the weather was bad. I explained that I didn't allow darts because of the danger of accidents. John said they would guarantee that no young ones were allowed in. He suggested that I give him keys so that he could keep the door locked. I refused saying that I had to have access to all rooms at all times.

On one occasion when I entered the room, I saw that John had a notice pinned on the wall. It was headed 'The Ten Commandments'. No 1 read: 'No…about!' I couldn't imagine anyone messing John around. However, I had no problems with John or his friends at any time. His team played all their outdoor soccer matches in hobnail boots. But they played as fairly as any of the other teams. On the other hand, John's language left a lot to be desired. I chastised him on numerous occasions for his use of bad language. On one occasion, he said, "I'm trying, Willie, I'm trying, but it is…hard to avoid it."

I suspected that John had some mental health problems which might have helped to explain why the other lads were afraid of him and always did what he said. My suspicions were confirmed when his team was beaten in the final of the soccer league. He went home and set fire to the house! I was talking to him sometime later and asked him what had got into him. He told me that his wife had been nagging at him all day because it was their wedding anniversary and all he was interested in was the final of the soccer competition. He said she had his 'head turned', so he blamed her when he didn't play well. He set fire to the house 'to teach her a lesson!'

Soon it was September again and the school reopened for another academic year. Up until now, *The Troubles* did not appear to have impacted to any significant extent on the pupils in St Peter's. Indeed we, the teachers, prided ourselves that our school provided an island of tranquillity where the pupils could be insulated for a few hours each day from The Troubles in the community. But our task became a great deal more difficult after the curfew as rioting got more widespread and young people got more involved.

Bombings, shootings, and rioting showed a marked increase during the school year 1970–71. It was impossible to shield the pupils from what was going on around them. I recall one evening I was driving home from school. I had just passed Casement Park when I realised that a bank robbery was taking place. It appeared that the Ulster Bank, situated where the Andersonstown Leisure Centre now stands, had just been held up. A car came screaming out onto the main road with a young man leaning out the window of the passenger door holding a revolver and shooting in all directions. It was like a scene from a film except this was for real as a bullet smashed through the windscreen of the car in front of me.

On another occasion, I was watering flowers in my front porch when I heard the rattle of machine-gun fire coming from the grounds of St Joseph's College. Two army vehicles had been going up the Andersonstown Road when they were ambushed by gunmen who were lying in wait in the college grounds. I watched as bullets cut a swathe across the field in front of my house heading in my direction. I stepped back from the window just in time as a bullet smashed through and shattered into smithereens against my bathroom wall.

The porch where I was standing was once open at the front and one side. The roof of the house extended over it. I had closed the front of the porch—the bottom half with wood and the top half with glass. I had also made a shelf where I could grow flowers. I put a new front door at the end of the porch for access to and from the driveway. This enclosed space now provided an extra room where our son could play during inclement weather and where my wife could sit when it was warmed by the sun. She suffered from multiple sclerosis and had to be carried out and in. Thankfully, neither of them was in the porch at that time. The bullet smashed through the wood at the front of the porch and hit what used to be the outside wall of the house, just below the bathroom window. It broke into small pieces. I gathered up the small pieces which looked like copper to me.

The gunmen, whom I assumed were members of the IRA, had been lying in wait in the undergrowth at a spot which is six or seven metres above the level of the road. The army scout cars were passing along the road below. The gunmen should have been pointing their guns down at the road. How had they managed to hit my house which was a couple of hundred metres away and on higher ground? Was it possible that it was the army who had fired the shots, one of which had hit my house? I decided to ask one of the pupils in St Peter's who seemed to have an unhealthy knowledge of the IRA and their weapons. I showed him the pieces of the bullet and asked him who had fired it. He laughed and said, "One of our lads" (meaning the IRA). I asked him how he knew. He said, "The army never uses them. The IRA don't either, but they are waiting for a supply of ammunition to come in. Those brass ones are all they have at the moment."

One day, I was going down the lane from my house, heading for the shop across the road. An army scout car was coming up the road approaching the traffic lights at the junction with Finaghy Road North and Andersonstown Road. As it passed the shop, a gunman stepped out from the side of St Michael's Church (which was still under construction) a few hundred metres away. He was holding a revolver and fired a few shots at the scout car before dodging back out of sight. The scout car had a Browning machine gun mounted on the turret. The soldiers opened fire with the machine gun, spraying the front of the church. The church still bears the scars of that assault. I thought it was absolutely crazy to use such a powerful gun in a built-up area. A .50BMG aimed round can hit a man-sized target 1.5-2 miles away. A round can travel 4–5 miles and still potentially cause injury if it strikes anyone. Firing such a gun in a built-up area showed total disregard for innocent people.

A row of shops, with flat roofs, to the north of my house appeared to be a favourite spot for IRA snipers. Presumably, they had a clear view of the junction of Finaghy Road North and the Andersonstown Road from the flat roof. I frequently saw tracer bullets as they fired at army patrols on the main road.

Once, the gunmen came a little too close for comfort. A high wall separates my house from the house next door and a lower wall stands on my side just opposite my side door. One evening as I was watching TV, I heard the rattle of machine-gun fire right beside the house. I went into the kitchen to see sparks flying past the kitchen window. I realised that the gunman was standing on my wall where he had a clear view of the Finaghy Road North-Andersonstown Road Junction less than 50 yards away.

Shortly afterwards, I heard hammering on my front door. It was the army wanting to search the house. The sergeant insisted that the shooting had come from upstairs. He demanded that I show him where the stairs were so that he could search there. He was most aggrieved when I told him that was not possible as I lived in a bungalow. He calmed down a little when I showed him where I thought the gunman had been, but he still wanted to search the house. I said he was welcome to do that so long as he did it under my guidance. He told me that he would take no directions from me as to where or what he would search. I told him I had an invalid wife in one room and a baby son in another, so he would search under my supervision or not at all. Surprisingly, he backed down. I took him into our bedroom where my wife was now awake. He had a quick look around but didn't disturb anything. I then took him into my son's room—he was sound asleep. Again, the sergeant looked quickly around and left quietly. He looked in my brother-in-law's room (he had been watching TV with me) and in the lounge. He had already been in the kitchen, so he apologised for disturbing us and left.

I was aware of the damage which was regularly caused to houses in Republican areas when being searched by the army—floorboards ripped up and doors smashed, for example. I was surprised by how lightly we had got off. On another occasion when they were searching in my garden, soldiers trampled flowers, broke bushes and damaged the fence. I complained to the commanding officer who said that if I provided a detailed list of everything which had been damaged, he would make sure that I received compensation. He kept his word. I could only surmise this was because I had been firm but polite.

Unrest in the province had reached a new level. The Rev Paisley was still hounding the Prime Minister to take more extreme action against the IRA. Chichester-Clark had been elected Prime Minister when Terence O'Neill resigned on 28 April 1969. He (Chichester-Clark) resigned in March 1971 and was replaced by Brian Faulkner. Five months later Faulkner decided to introduce internment—to arrest and hold people without evidence, to take them off the streets and prevent further murders. The RUC claimed that they knew who the main members of the terrorist organisations were.

342 people suspected of supporting paramilitaries were arrested in the first swoop. During the round-up operation in West Belfast from 9 to 11 August, the Parachute Regiment killed 11 unarmed civilians within 100 yards of St Peter's Secondary School in what became known as the *Ballymurphy Massacre.* Fourteen civilians in total were shot dead by the British army, and three security forces personnel were shot dead by republicans. In the following days, an estimated 7000 people fled their homes. The vast majority of those killed, imprisoned, or forced to flee were nationalists and Catholics.

Once again, St Peter's School was full of refugees— mainly terrified women and children. I decided to get the school minibus and ferry some of them to the railway station from where they were travelling by rail to various locations in the Irish Republic. I had two five-gallon drums filled with diesel in my car going up the Whiterock Road when I was stopped by an army patrol. The soldiers wanted to know where I was going. I didn't really expect them to let me through, especially being loaded down with diesel. I explained what I was doing and said it was essential that I got as many women and children out of danger as possible. The soldiers told me that I was crazy because there was heavy shooting in the vicinity of the school—if I went on it would be at my own risk. The relief on the faces of the women and children, when I got them to the station, made it all worthwhile.

Within six months, 2357 people had been interned, 90% from the Nationalist community and 10% from the loyalist community. 1600 of these were subsequently released without charge. The whole procedure was badly organised. Flawed 'police intelligence' was probably based on lists supplied by the Rev Paisley's *Ulster Protestant Action*. Many innocent people were detained while most of the leaders of the terrorist organisations slipped through the net.

Internment was a disaster, both in its failure to capture any significant members of the IRA and in its focus on nationalist—rather than on both nationalist and loyalist—suspects. Intended to nip the insurrection in the bud, in effect it added fuel to the flames.

The reaction to internment was predictable, even if the ferocity and extent of the violence weren't. Deaths in the final months of 1971 exceeded 150. Policing the province was fast becoming an impossible task, and as a result, the British army adopted increasingly aggressive policies on the ground. Then on 30 January 1972, the army deployed the Parachute Regiment to suppress rioting at a civil rights march in Derry. Thirteen demonstrators were shot and killed by troops, with another dying later of wounds, in what became known as *Bloody Sunday*. As a result of the killings, new recruits swelled the ranks of the IRA, and yet more British troops were deployed to the province to try and contain the ever-rising tide of violence.

Some of the boys in St Peter's were now openly involved in the Fianna (junior IRA). They could be seen acting as 'Guards of Honour' at the republican funerals which were passing up Falls Road on the way to Milltown Cemetery almost daily. Some were involved in rioting and hijackings.

One day, one of the boys asked if he could talk to me in private. He told me that a boy in his class had a revolver and ammunition in his school bag. The teacher who would be taking the class for the next lesson was well known for physically abusing boys in the class who were misbehaving. Sometimes he used his fists, but he would also kick them when he got really angry. The boy who had the gun was often on the receiving end. My informant was concerned that he might be planning to shoot the teacher.

I got this information at the morning break and was able to contact the boy with the gun before lessons restarted. I asked him to tell me why he had brought a gun into school. He told me that he was on active service. The IRA planned to move a cache of guns from one location to another in the Springfield Road area that morning. The boy had been instructed to slip out of school and go to a named location. At a set time, he was to fire a few shots in the air. Army personnel would rush to where they heard the gunfire while the IRA would transfer the guns to the new location.

I was chastising the boy for taking the gun in his schoolbag and putting himself and others in danger going to and from school and himself in more danger by firing shots to draw the army away from the IRA. What if a sniper spotted him? It might be the last thing he would do. Suddenly he said, "F…you, Willie. You have kept me late. There is no point in going now." I told him not to bring a gun into school again.

I remember once driving down the Falls Road in the evening with my wife. As we approached the Falls Road/Grosvenor Road junction, we suddenly found ourselves in the middle of a riot. Cars were being stopped and the drivers were told to get out so that the cars could be used as barricades. We were surrounded in seconds and there was no possibility of escape. Suddenly someone shouted, "It's wee Willie, leave him alone." A group of boys from St Peter's cleared a space for me to get the car turned. They advised me to be more careful the next time and waved me on my way. I was grateful that I had such a good relationship with my pupils.

Insulating the boys from violence was no longer an option—violence was all around them. 'Normal' life was far from normal. It was not unusual to find a soldier lying across my doorway pointing a rifle at nothing in particular. On occasion, I would have to step over a soldier to get out and then lean back over him to close the door.

Once, I spotted a soldier lying in my front garden firing shots through my side garden gate at a row of houses some distance across the field. I heard no return fire, so I went out to ask him what he was doing. He looked around and asked, "Do you know where that shot came from?" I replied that if he didn't know, he shouldn't be firing. I pointed out that children were on their way to school and had to cross his line of fire. If he kept shooting some child was likely to get killed. He agreed, stood up, called the other members of his patrol and they moved on.

I tried to keep my son Liam out of harm's way to the extent possible. Then one day, he managed to slip my attention. I looked out the kitchen window to see him standing talking to a soldier who was lying on the grass with his rifle pointing out the side garden gate. Liam was about three at the time. I went out to bring him in and noted that tears were streaming down the soldier's face. I asked him what was wrong. He told me he was from Scotland. He had a son about the same age as Liam and he missed him terribly. I asked him why he had joined the army. He said it was impossible to find work in Glasgow—it was either the army or the dole queue. I said I hoped he would soon get home safe to his wife and son.

The violence was all around us, inside or outside of the house. I recall walking up Andersonstown Road with Liam past a number of lorries and cars which had been hijacked and set on fire to prevent army vehicles from getting through. I was walking along chatting to Liam trying to pretend that this was a normal afternoon stroll. Suddenly he burst into tears. I asked him what was wrong, and he pointed to a burning lorry. I said, "You have seen burning lorries before, why is that one upsetting you?"

He replied, "Because it is a Lucozade lorry and Lucozade is for making sick people better!" I guessed he was thinking about his mother, as Lucozade was her favourite drink. I told him not to worry, there would be plenty more in the shops.

The boys in St Peter's, too, were growing up with violence. Some were involved in creating it—hijacking cars and buses and stoning the army. But they didn't have to be actively involved to get caught up in it. Rubber bullets were used for the first time on 2 August 1970, and children were the target more frequently than adults. Their use was controversial at the time and has remained so ever since.

Children didn't really understand how dangerous rubber bullets could be, and the soldiers didn't care. On 22 April 1972, an 11-year-old boy, walking through the Divis Flats complex, in the centre of St Peter's parish, close to Belfast's Falls Road, was hit on the head by a rubber bullet fired by a soldier for no apparent reason. He died two days later. The soldier identified as the one who fired the shot denied he had even been there. He said he would remember the incident if he had been. When evidence was presented at the Coroner's Court that he had fired the shot, he said there must have been serious rioting because he always played by the book. He was a sergeant major and always believed in setting a good example for his men. He refused to accept that there was no riot.

On 4 May 1972, 10-year-old Richard Moore and his friend were on their way home from Rosemount Primary School in Derry. There was an army look-out post situated near the school which they had to pass twice a day every school day. As they came up to the look-out post on 4 May, a senior army officer, a captain in the British Royal Artillery regiment, fired a rubber bullet and hit Richard Moore on the bridge of the nose, leaving him blind for life.

Later investigations revealed that the child was less than ten feet away when the shot was fired. The Ministry of Defence released a statement which said the post was being attacked by a crowd of youths throwing stones at the time of the incident. The captain, apparently unaware of the MOD statement, said he fired the shot to frighten the two children away as he didn't want them playing too close to the look-out post. He admitted that he hadn't gone out to examine the child after he fired the shot.

Richard Moore is now the director of the Derry-based charity Children in Crossfire. His charity was recently awarded a £250,000 UK government grant through the Department for International Development's UK Aid Direct scheme to help provide 100,000 children in the Dodoma region of Tanzania with an education.

In 2007, he met the soldier who shot him and has forgiven him. He has since maintained a friendship with the soldier.

The Dalai Lama is a patron of Mr Moore's Children in Crossfire charity.

The gun used for firing rubber (and later plastic) bullets (also referred to as baton rounds) was invented by army engineers for use in Northern Ireland and was designed to deter people from rioting by hurting but not killing them.

The BBC Spotlight programme, 'Lethal: The Secret History of Plastic Bullets' shown on BBC 1, Northern Ireland on Tuesday, 14 March 2023, at 10.40 pm reveals how documents showed that the gun the RUC was using was never fully cleared for use against people.

The British army's own Land Operations Manual stated that baton rounds should not be used against children. But this instruction was never passed on to soldiers. At least, 120,000 rounds were fired during The Troubles.

Seventeen people have been killed in Northern Ireland by members of the security forces who were using rubber or plastic bullets and others suffered serious injuries, including brain damage and blinding. Sixteen of the seventeen killed were Catholics. Eight of the sixteen Catholics killed were children.

Chapter 12
Skating on Thin Ice

Following the riots of 1969, residents, and paramilitaries, built barricades in some places to seal-off and protect their neighbourhoods from incursions by 'the other side', by the security forces, or both. These areas were patrolled by militant residents and became known as 'no-go' areas. The introduction of internment in August 1971 led to an upsurge in support for the IRA and reinforcement of these areas. Andersonstown, where I lived, was a 'no-go' area.

Most streets leading into the Andersonstown estate were barricaded. One access and exit point for vehicular traffic to the estate was via the private lane leading up to my house. At that time, there was a field directly in front of my house with a stream running down the middle. A fence separated my lane from the field. The IRA made a gap in the fence just opposite my front gate to allow access across the top of the field and into the Andersonstown estate. To say that I was annoyed would be an understatement. No one had bothered to ask me. Now I had a steady flow of cars and lorries streaming up and down my lane. It was nearly impossible to get out of my front gate.

After one week, I had had enough. I decided to close and seal the gap in front of my house and prevent access to the field and hence to the estate. I knew I would be locking horns with the IRA, but I had news for them which I was sure would win them over.

I was up early on Saturday morning, knowing that the traffic would be light. I had a couple of heavy posts, some sand and cement to make sure they would not be easy to remove, and some barbed wire. I was expecting company and didn't have long to wait. I was busy digging holes for the posts when I heard someone asking what I thought I was doing. I looked up to see two strangers standing beside me. I guessed they were IRA and the bulging right-hand pockets suggested that they were both armed. I said that the Andersonstown estate was wide open to attack. I was sealing a glaring loophole. They asked me who had given me permission. I said there hadn't been time to ask anyone for permission. The matter was too urgent.

I knew they wouldn't swallow that without a more detailed account. I explained that I had been in a pub in Dunmurry the previous night. I said that I had observed a group at an adjoining table and recognised one of the ladies as being 'Orange Lilly'[17]. They were all listening intently to what she was saying. I listened too. She explained that of all the 'no-go areas', Andersonstown was the easiest to access. All they had to do was drive up Finaghy Road North, cross the road and drive up the lane almost directly opposite, cross the top of the field and into the estate. She claimed that she had driven into the estate herself, driven around and back out

---

[17] A Shankill Road Radio Personality.

again. No one had noticed. She laughed as she told them they could drive in, plant a bomb and be back in Dunmurry before it exploded.

The two IRA men were listening attentively to me. They thanked me profusely for my alertness and quick action. Did I need anyone to give me a hand? I said I was quite happy to get on with the work myself. They were concerned that the attack from Dunmurry might come early and promised that at least one of them would stay on guard all day, hiding behind the hedge, to ensure that I got the gap closed and sealed. I wasn't sure whether to be amused or apprehensive about having an armed guard as I worked. I don't know when exactly they left. All I can say is that there was no sign of them when I was clearing up in the evening.

During the time the 'no-go areas' were operational, the IRA were comfortable in the knowledge that they were in control and that they 'policed' those areas. Hence their willingness to let people know that they were armed. It wasn't sufficient to control the areas. They wanted everyone to know who was in charge.

Ballymurphy was also a no-go area at this time, and it was necessary to make a slight detour to gain access to St Peter's School. On one occasion, I was driving to the school, following the obligatory diversions. As I rounded a corner, there was John sitting on the footpath surrounded by his gang. He had a revolver in his hand, and he was, apparently, showing the group how to load it or clean it or both.

On another occasion, I was on my way to open the school for the evening classes. As I approached the same spot, I saw John standing on the footpath. He waved me down and asked if I would give him a lift over to his house. I said, "What do you want a lift for, John, it's only about 100 yards?" I leaned over and opened the door to let him in. He reached down and pulled a rifle out of the hedge. I said, "John, you will get me shot, or I will end up in prison."

One day while working in the summer scheme, I got a message from one of the (community service) grannies that she would like to see me. I heard the rattle of machine-gun fire as I left the school. The shooting appeared to be in the street close to where 'Granny' lived. I stopped a man and asked him what was going on. He told me that someone was firing a Gatling gun and the bullets were bouncing off the wall around Corry's Timber Yard. This was a favourite spot used by army and loyalist snipers and probably the vantage point used by the snipers responsible for the *Ballymurphy Massacre*. I could only imagine that the men with the Gatling gun were attempting to breach the wall. The next time I passed that way, I noted that the wall was pockmarked—but still standing.

Granny was well, despite what sounded like a gun battle nearby. I reassured her that the 'gun battle' was just some men practising and she was in no danger. She wanted some things from the shop. I arranged to get them delivered to her.

I recall one occasion when the IRA carried out an audacious raid on a container ship in Belfast docks and drove off with half a dozen brand-new unregistered cars. Rumour had it that the cars were given false number plates and used as 'staff' cars by local commanders. One of the cars was a white Mercedes. The commander in Andersonstown apparently considered that he was the senior commander in Belfast. He insisted that he should have the Mercedes. He should have known that there wasn't another white Mercedes in Andersonstown. The police picked 'his' car up the next day. The other five cars were all Ford Cortinas and were driven around for months before the police got them.

A more usual method of obtaining transport for the IRA was to steal or hijack private cars. Now that they regarded themselves as the local police force, they decided that they had the right to 'borrow' cars as and when they needed them. They realised that they had access to a ready supply of 'clean' cars in the car parks of the local schools. It became routine for children to knock on a classroom door and tell the teacher that 'a man in the car park wants to borrow your car keys'. Refusal risked the possibility that 'the man' would take your car anyway. In that case, the car was unlikely to be returned and would probably be found burnt somewhere.

The IRA were so full of confidence that they were openly drilling at this time. Once, I opened the school for the evening classes to find the gym full of men drilling. I ordered them out and said I hoped not to find them in the school again. Surprisingly, they left. I suspected that the caretaker had let them in but realised the pressure he was under living in the midst of them.

From time to time, I got requests in the evening for the use of a room for a meeting. I would find a group of men at the door claiming to be residents wanting to organise things to assist people in the community who couldn't help themselves. I had no way of knowing whether they were legitimate community leaders or members of a paramilitary group. I let them in but tried to keep an eye on them to make sure that nothing untoward was going on.

One day during the summer scheme, I was told that two snipers wearing balaclavas were observed on the roof of the school. I climbed onto the roof and ordered them to get down. I pointed out that if they started shooting from the school, the police, soldiers or loyalists would inevitably fire back. The schoolyard was full of children. Some of them were liable to get killed. The two snipers must have thought I was crazy. I would be the first one to get hit if shooting started. I was a perfect target, standing upright on the roof. Despite my haranguing, they refused to come down. They said they would not open fire unless they were fired on first. I was increasing that possibility by drawing attention to them.

As I argued with the gunmen, I saw two men running across the front of the school, one carrying a five-gallon drum and the other carrying a ladder. They placed the ladder against the wall of Corry's Timber Yard, and one climbed up. He emptied the contents of the drum over a stack of timber, lit a piece of cloth and tossed it onto the pile. Flames shot high into the air and the two men raced back across the front of the school—mission accomplished. Then, as quickly as they started, the flames went out. Clearly, Corry's had anticipated such an attack and had treated the timber with fire retardant. The two snipers got down off the roof and all four disappeared back into the estate.

St Peter's Immaculata Youth Centre in the Lower Falls area of Belfast had a great reputation for producing top-class boxers. Consequently, we had a lot of boys in the school who were interested in boxing. Frequently, I found that the boys from the D-streams were the most talented. Each year I borrowed a boxing ring and the relevant equipment and organised a boxing competition so that these boys had an opportunity to show off their skills. Michael, Head of the Metalwork Department, was a former All-Ireland boxing champion. We were close friends and he always helped. The competition ran for four weeks. For the rest of the year, the borrowed equipment was returned to the owners and whatever we owned was stored under the stage. It was competition time again and some of the boys were helping me to put the ring up. I asked them to get the equipment from under the stage. One boy came back and whispered that there was a 'pile' of rifles down there. I asked him if he knew the leader of the IRA in the Ballymurphy area and where he lived. He said he did. I said, "Go and tell him I want the guns removed immediately." I told the boys who had been under the stage not to mention the guns to anyone. I didn't ask how many guns there were or check any other details.

Later that day, a man called and said he had come to collect the guns. I still had my team with me erecting the boxing ring. One of the boys told me the man was from the 'Official' IRA. I wasn't prepared to get into a dispute between the two factions of the IRA. I said I couldn't let him take the guns because someone had already been told to pick them up. He replied that they had an arrangement. In a situation like this, either branch of the IRA could pick guns up to prevent the army or the police from getting them. I didn't know how I was going to stop him if he insisted on taking them— particularly, if he was armed. But he didn't insist. He just left. No one else called before the school closed. The guns were gone the next morning.

The existence of 'no-go areas' was a challenge to the authority of the British in Northern Ireland. *Operation Motorman* took place in the early hours of 31 July 1972 with the aim of retaking these areas. This was the biggest British military operation since the Suez Crisis of 1956 and the biggest in Ireland since the Irish War of Independence. The army used bulldozers and several Centurion tanks to break through the barricades in the Bogside before flooding the areas with troops. The barricades in Belfast were more easily demolished.

Once the barricades were demolished, the army re-established control. In many areas, for example, the Bogside in Derry, the Falls Road, and Ardoyne in Belfast, while the official status was removed, the status of a no-go area remained in operation, with the police and army personnel only entering in certain circumstances, namely a combatant role or house raids. Ballymurphy, however, came under the direct control of the army when they seized control of St Peter's School. We couldn't believe it when we were informed that a company of 'the Parachute Regiment' would be sharing the school with us. We objected strongly, insisting that they were effectively using teachers and children as human shields as the IRA would be reluctant to open fire on the school. It was to no avail. The soldiers took over approximately one-third of the school—including my office!

Tensions were high in the school. It was not a good atmosphere for teaching. Everyone resented the presence of the soldiers. The teachers feared for the safety of the children, and themselves of course, lest the IRA would decide to launch a rocket at the school or open fire on army patrols entering or leaving the school premises.

Tensions reached a breaking point when the officer commanding decided that we all had to be checked upon entering the school each morning and informed us that they reserved the right to search our belongings and our persons. The right to search was extended to the children also. We reminded them that it was our school—they were the uninvited guests, but they weren't listening. We complained to the Department of Education, but they insisted it was out of their hands.

We were stopped at the school gate each morning, had to produce a driving licence or other ID, and had our briefcases and other bags searched. One morning I arrived to find that one of the staff was being refused admission. I was allowed through. I parked my car and went over to enquire what the problem was. I informed the sergeant that the man concerned was one of our staff. He told me in old English to mind my own business. I told him it was my business since he was refusing admission to one of our teachers. He warned me that if I didn't clear off, I would be arrested. I knew that they had been given a typed list of all members of staff. I was also aware that some of the soldiers were barely literate. I asked him to let me see the list and said I would find the teacher's name for him. The sergeant exploded, saying that he had had enough of me. He grabbed me by the left arm and ordered another soldier to take me by the right arm. They began ushering me towards the gate to throw me out. The sergeant was about 6ft 3ins tall and the soldier was about 5ft 10ins. I was just under 5ft 6ins. So, there wasn't much point in my resisting.

Instead, I ran with them as quickly as I could towards the gate. The gate opened at a 90° angle to the surrounding wall. As we reached the gate, I stepped suddenly to the left to go inside the gate instead of outside. Both the sergeant and the soldier were taken by surprise. The soldier stumbled, hit his head on the gate and fell to the ground stunned. The sergeant exploded with rage, released my arm, and grabbed his rifle by the barrel. He was about to hit me across the back of my head with the butt when the commanding officer roared at him to stop. Lucky for me, someone had gone to inform the principal about the argument in the car park. The principal had summoned the major and the major had arrived in the nick of time to save me from, at best, a very sore head. The major offered his sincere apologies for the incident. He was highly amused that these two big men from such an elite regiment had been unable to get me out through the gate. He asked me if I would like to join his company!

The principal mentioned above was our second principal, a very different man from the first who was an outstanding academic. Our second principal was intent on building a name for himself as a strict disciplinarian. He enforced discipline with corporal punishment. He announced that anyone who was sent to him wouldn't want to be sent a second time. Those who were sent a second time were taken up on stage during morning assembly so that all the pupils could witness the punishment.

I don't believe that corporal punishment solves anything. And I thought that it was most inappropriate to administer it during assembly when we all come together for morning prayer. It was like a public execution. Besides, the principal didn't seem to appreciate that punishment had as little impact as throwing water over a duck. Many of these boys came from violent home backgrounds where beatings were a regular occurrence.

While displaying a hard-man approach when doling out punishment to pupils during morning assembly, the principal kept his head down when staff members were having problems with the soldiers in the car park. He was always too busy in his office to come out. When someone went to tell him that things were getting out of hand in my case, he called the major but didn't come out himself.

Still, he came to me on one occasion and asked if I would take over a class where the regular teacher was in hospital as a result of a nervous breakdown. I wasn't sure whether he believed the class was beyond control and wanted to see me fail or whether he really believed that I was the only one who could settle the pupils down and get them to do some real work.

I asked the boys what they had been up to. They told me that the teacher came in every day threatening to slap the whole class if they didn't settle down. They didn't. He would make them all stand in a line and start slapping. They would take their slaps and then join the back of the queue and go round a second, and sometimes a third time. The teacher slapped away until he was exhausted. I asked how long this had gone on for. They said it only took a couple of weeks before he had a nervous breakdown. They added that they had been trying to decide who to take on next. Then I came in and spoiled it. But behind all the bravado, they had clearly been bored because they settled down quickly for me and produced some excellent work before the end of the year. There was disbelief amongst fellow staff members, and the principal when they saw samples of work displayed around the room. The boys carefully took their work down to take home with them. There wasn't a red biro mark in sight.[18]

---

[18] To find out how I achieved this, see p187 of *Big Boys don't Cry* An Autobiography by Dr Willie McCarney, published by Matador, 2015. Available as an ebook.

I was surprised a second time when the principal came to me and asked if I could provide him with a detailed report of the Community Service project, the summer school scheme, and the night classes. I explained that I had not prepared a report yet because all of the projects were 'work in progress'. He said he was sure that I could prepare an excellent report and would be very pleased if I would do that for him. He said he would be attending a very important meeting and would like to promote St Peter's by outlining the range of projects being undertaken by the school.

I would find out later that the principal was planning to use the report to promote himself and not the school. He claimed that he was behind all the projects, even though he had not even been in the school when I launched them. As a result, he got himself elected to an important committee which, in turn, led to his appointment to a highly-paid job—a much more lucrative position than school principal. I never suspected that he could be so deceitful or that the reason he wanted my report so desperately was that he planned to use it for his own ends. Once he got what he wanted, he left.

I don't know what the major said to his men, following the incident I was involved in, but there were no more incidents regarding admission to the school. Nonetheless, tensions remained high since everyone believed that, sooner or later, the IRA would attempt to pick off one of the soldiers. Sure enough, one lunchtime, when the yard was full of children playing, two shots rang out. The bullets struck the school wall and ricocheted across the yard. All the staff agreed that we should not continue to teach in the school while the army remained in it. The principal rang the

Department of Education to inform them of our decision. The children got an unexpected holiday.

The solution which the department came up with was to have us housed in various locations in the Lower Falls. All the primary schools in St Peter's parish were asked to accommodate as many classes as possible. Eight classes were to be accommodated in Clonard Hall (in the grounds of Clonard Monastery). I was designated 'Principal' of Clonard Hall.

Clonard Hall was quite a change from St Peter's. The boys were more subdued. I couldn't quite put my finger on the reason. Perhaps they had been traumatised by the shooting incident in St Peter's. But they must have experienced many shooting and bombing incidents and there must have been many times when shots came too close for comfort. Perhaps, like us, they saw the school as an island of tranquillity in the ocean of violence which surrounded us all. That illusion had been shaken when the army took over our school and claimed it as their base in Ballymurphy. The illusion had been shattered when the IRA decided that it was now a legitimate target. But the explanation might have been more mundane. The numbers in Clonard Hall were much smaller than the main school. So, there were fewer malcontents. Besides, I had a good relationship with all of the boys, and they generally listened when I spoke.

There were only two incidents worth recording in the few months we were in Clonard Hall. The first was a serious fight between two of the senior boys. There was nothing unusual about fights. They happened all the time. The boys were always slagging one another and sometimes the slagging went too far and ended in fisticuffs. But this was different. The onlookers realised it and one of them came running to get me. When I arrived on the scene, I found that the bigger of the two boys had grabbed a lemonade bottle and broken it. He was holding what was left of it by the neck and was intent on slashing the other boy with the wicked-looking shards of glass which were still attached.

I shouted to him to leave the bottle down. He didn't respond to me. He kept repeating, "I'm going to kill him; I'm going to kill him." I don't know what the other boy had said to him, but I knew that many of these boys came from troubled family backgrounds, and many had skeletons in the cupboard which were not discussed. Whatever had been said left this young man literally crazy with anger. I could tell by his eyes that he really meant what he said. He really did intend to kill the other boy if he could get hold of him. The other boy realised that, too. He was ashen-faced as he tried to dodge the thrusts and parries of that broken bottle. He was afraid to turn and run lest he would be stabbed in the back.

The pupil with the bottle was a big lad but I knew I was going to have to stop him somehow. I thought he respected me enough not to stab me with the bottle. Still, I wasn't sure that it was safe to try to get between him and his quarry and wrestle the bottle from him. I ran up behind him, locked my arms around him pinning his arms by his sides. He struggled violently to get free, but I hung on like grim death. My arms were aching. I thought I would never be able to hold on until he calmed down. I don't know how long I hung on for. It seemed like an eternity to me but probably was no more than five minutes, ten at the outside.

At last, the boy relaxed and promised to give me the broken bottle if I let him go. He was sobbing violently. I took him into my office and sat chatting to him for a while. I asked him if he would like to tell me what happened and he said he would rather not, at least not now. I enquired whether he would shake hands with the other boy if the other boy apologised. He said he would, so I called the other boy in. He apologised, they shook hands and the two boys left. They never told me what had been said which triggered the violent outburst.

The other incident was more mundane. One of the teachers brought Liam to my office. I asked him what the problem was, and he told me that Liam had been misbehaving in class. I asked him why he hadn't dealt with it himself. He said he didn't believe in corporal punishment, so he was leaving that job for me. I said that I thought his philosophy was a little muddled up if he was personally opposed to corporal punishment while, at the same time, asking me to slap Liam on his behalf. He didn't answer that. I told him to leave Liam with me.

I asked Liam to sit down as I was completing some important papers. He was busy fidgeting in his seat, and I asked him what was wrong. He replied that he would prefer if I got on with the punishment and let him get back to class. I asked him what punishment he was expecting, and he replied, "The usual six slaps, I suppose." I said the slaps didn't appear to be doing any good as he was always in trouble. He agreed. I said I had decided not to punish him at all. I had a job for him to do instead. I had to deliver these papers to an office downtown. It was a criminal offence in Northern Ireland at that time to leave your car unattended outside of an official car park. It would only take me a couple of minutes to deliver the papers, and I needed to get back to the school quickly.

Would he come with me and sit in the car while I ran into the office? He said he would.

I really wanted to get Liam on his own for a while in a relaxed atmosphere and try to get to the bottom of his misbehaviour. On our way downtown, I asked him if he could explain why he was always in trouble with most teachers. To my surprise, he burst into tears. When he finished crying, he began to tell me about his home life.

Liam told me that he was the eldest of eight children. His father had walked out, and his mother was an alcoholic. Liam's day began bright and early. He got the baby up, changed its nappy and gave it a bottle. Then he got his brothers and sisters up, washed, dressed and ready for school. He brought his mother a cup of tea—if she was awake. He got his brothers and sisters out to school, wrapped the baby up and left it with his granny who lived nearby. Then he headed off to school himself. In the evenings, he would collect the baby, make everyone their dinner, and get the others to do their homework. By the time he had them all organised and off to bed, he was ready to collapse into bed himself.

There wasn't much time in Liam's day for homework. The amazing thing was that he bothered going to school at all. And yet he never missed a day even though he knew he was in for a beating. I let the other teachers know that Liam deserved a medal and not punishment. The beatings stopped.

Much of my stuff was still in St Peter's, so I had to go up there from time to time. The officer commanding (the major who had saved me from the beating) had taken up residence in my office and had no worries about letting me in to collect my stuff. I noticed that he had a photo of Michael, the IRA commander in Ballymurphy, on the wall with the caption:

'Wanted, Dead or Alive'. Sometime later I heard that they had got their man. I wondered about John who had attended the summer school. I was told that he was coming home from the pub one night and was stopped by an army patrol on Whiterock Road. They gave him a severe beating and then flung him over the wall into the City Cemetery where they left him for dead. I understand that he was still alive when found the next morning but don't know if he ever recovered from his injuries.

The soldiers knew me and didn't bother coming out of the sangar[19] to check for ID or to search me. They were generally surrounded by copies of the Sun but never seemed to get past page 3. This tended to confirm my earlier view that literacy was not their strong point.

On one of my visits to the school, I learned from the major that they would soon be moving out. The army had been given permission to commission our playing fields at McCrory Park and to build an army barracks there. The construction would be done very quickly and would allow them to vacate the school. I was disappointed to hear that we were losing our playing field but happy to hear that we would be getting our school back. Fort Pegasus became operational around Christmas 1972, and we were back in our school at the beginning of January 1973.

We were back to the old routine with constant concerns about the children's safety as they had to walk past Fort

---

[19] A sangar is a temporary fortified position with a breastwork originally constructed of stones, and now built of sandbags, gabions, or similar materials. Sangars are normally constructed in terrain where the digging of trenches would not be practicable.

Pegasus on their way to and from school. One evening, a stranger called into the school and told me to finish the evening classes early. The IRA had planned to attack Fort Pegasus and didn't want staff or students from the evening classes caught up in the attack. I said I couldn't close early. How would I explain that I knew about the attack in advance but hadn't informed the army or the police?

There was no attack on the fort that night. I wondered whether my refusal to cooperate had influenced the IRA's decision not to launch an attack. Was it possible that I had saved lives? I would never know. It was inevitable that attacks would resume. The military suffered its first casualty there when a soldier was killed during an IRA attack on the Fort in February 1973.

Shootings, bombings, and rioting continued with the boys more involved in the Fianna (the junior IRA) than ever. It was becoming increasingly clear to me that some of the older boys were involved in 'active service'. One of the A-level boys came in with his hand bandaged. He told me that he had been watching an army sniper through a pair of binoculars. The sniper was lining up on something or someone. He wondered what. Suddenly his binoculars shattered, and he realised that the top of his index finger had been shot off. The sniper had been lining up on him. He said he was so lucky to be standing talking to me. He denied being on 'active service' and insisted that he was 'just being nosey'.

There was no internationally accepted definition of what constituted 'a child' until the UN's 1989 Convention on the Rights of the Child (the CRC) defined 'a child' as anyone under the age of 18. There was no international law banning the use of 'Child Soldiers' until the CRC's Optional Protocol came into effect in 2002. Nonetheless, it was generally accepted, even in the early 1970s, that children should not be engaged in armed combat.

As reports of other incidents, like the two mentioned above, were beginning to filter back to me I began to reflect on the goals I had set myself when I came to St Peter's. I set out to convince the school authorities that success should not be measured solely by the number of children achieving O-levels and A-levels but by the extent to which the teachers help all children to be the best they can be. I had clearly failed to achieve this. I had failed to convince the education authorities that the curriculum needed to be changed and I failed to convince the teachers that they needed to change their teaching methods.

But what about the D-stream boys? Had I failed them? They came to me already labelled as failures, sent to the 'school for failures' because they had failed, (or had failed to sit) the eleven-plus (11+). On arrival at the 'school for failures', they failed to be selected for the A-stream; failed to be selected for the B-stream and failed to be selected for the C-stream. What about the D-stream? They weren't selected for the D-stream. That is where they found themselves, at the bottom of the pile—the dregs of academia. The boys put it more simply. They were the dunces. They felt they had been clearly labelled: 'Good for nothing'.

My aim was to help them to develop self-confidence, a belief in themselves, a belief that they had talents which could be developed. Together we could get them back on the road to becoming the best they could be. The aim of the summer scheme was to occupy their time during the long summer holidays so that they were less likely to get into trouble. The evening classes provided them with opportunities to improve their skills and make them better fitted for the world of work. The community service projects were intended to improve their self-esteem by helping those less fortunate than themselves.

There was still work to be done but now the ball was in their own hands. They could achieve something better if they put their minds to it. I had pushed them to the limits of physical fitness through the activities in the gym, on the football field and in the mountains. As far as I could see, they were well prepared for the road ahead.

But there were forces out there which were beyond my control, and which had attractions I couldn't match. The IRA enticed them into the Fianna with promises of increased status. They would be today's heroes fighting to drive the British out of Ireland. Tomorrow's songs would be about them:

> *Heads erect, eyes in front stepping proudly together;*
>
> *...*
>
> *strong manly forms, eyes with hope gleaming;*
>
> *...*
>
> *they stood by old Ireland and never feared danger;*
>
> *...*
>
> *It was one last push for a United Ireland.*

Those who decided to join the Fianna served their apprenticeship hijacking cars and buses and taking the front line in riots. For some, the apprenticeship was short. On 9 March 1972, I woke up to the news that there had been an explosion in a vacant house on Clonard Street. The police said that four of the IRA's top bomb experts had been making a bomb. The bomb exploded prematurely. The boys told me that one of the four was a former pupil of mine in (St Peter's), now aged about 16. There were two 19-year-olds and one aged 20. They were mixing materials for a fertiliser bomb. I was told that they were using ordinary shovels as if they were mixing sand and cement to make concrete. I knew nothing about making fertiliser bombs, but I imagined that a more scientific approach would have been required. If that story was true, they were hardly bomb experts.

I was saddened to hear that another of my past pupils had been shot. It was the boy I told you about in my report from Clonard Hall. It was a sad end for Liam who had deserved a gold medal for the way he looked after his family, taking on the dual role of father and mother. He had apparently taken on the role of sniper. I couldn't imagine how he had gained sufficient experience with a rifle to be able to graduate as a sniper. I was told that he was trying to line up on a target when an army sniper got him.

For the past eight years, I had been ready to protect them against all comers. I walked the middle ground, neither on one side nor the other. The police and the soldiers were professionals. They could look after themselves. I was not supporting the IRA. I was not taking orders from them. And I was not going to be used by them. I saw my role as protecting the young people in my care. I regularly found myself dicing with death knowing that, if I put a foot wrong, I could disappear without trace—for example, when I ordered the snipers to get off the roof; when I ordered IRA members to get out of the school having found them drilling in the sports hall; when I left orders that guns found under the stage were to be removed before the school opened next morning; when I refused an order from the IRA to close the school early because they were planning an attack on the army barracks at the end of the street. I never knew why they took orders from me. I can only assume that they decided I was an honest broker and that my entire focus was on the best interests of the children. I sometimes wondered whether I had been wrong in adopting that approach.

I remember confiding in my good friend Fred Milson, a Methodist Minister, Principal Lecturer and Head of Department at Westhill College (the old Methodist Teacher Education College—later to be renamed Birmingham University, Westhill). I thought my situation was unique. To my surprise, Fred responded, "Far from it." Fred had done some work in Algeria following *The Algerian War of Independence*[20] which ended with the signing of the Evian Accords in March 1962. He said that some of the people he worked with in Algiers told him they had been faced with a similar dilemma and had come to the same conclusion. It was reassuring to know that others shared my views.

Years later, as I travelled the world on 'missions' for the UN, the UNDP, UNICEF, and the Council of Europe, I got further confirmation that my dilemma was not unique. Many people working with children in conflict situations choose what they believe to be in the best interests of the children.

---

[20] The Algerian War of Independence was a major armed conflict between France and the Algerian National Liberation Front which lasted from 1954 to 1962. The war ended with the signing of the Evian Accords in March 1962 which led to Algeria winning its independence from French colonial rule.

Chapter 13
ROSLA Highlighted the
Need for Change

I set out to give readers some idea of what it was like trying to fulfil the educational needs of children while being mindful of their social and emotional needs. There is also a need to provide children with a place of safety, remote from the bloody guerrilla war, which was raging around them, frequently consuming their homes, their family, and their friends. At the same time, the teachers had to be aware of the needs of their own families, while getting to grips with significant changes in the educational field. I have covered the introduction of secondary modern schools in some detail. I now want to consider the impact of the raising of the school leaving age (ROSLA[21]) to 16 in 1972.

---

[21] **ROSLA** (the **R**aising **O**f the **S**chool **L**eaving **A**ge) is the term used by the United Kingdom government for changes to the age at which a child is allowed to leave compulsory education. Compulsory education was initially introduced for 5- to 10-year-olds, in England and Wales, in 1880. The leaving age was increased to 11 in 1893, 12 in 1899, 14 in 1918, 15 in 1947 and 16 in 1972. This was increased in England to 17 in 2013 and 18 in 2015.

ROSLA had a dramatic impact on secondary schools, particularly those without sixth forms, which were obliged to provide pupils with a suitable curriculum for the additional year of their schooling. It was understood that an additional year of schooling 'should offer new and challenging courses' instead of just being a continuation of what had been taught before.

ROSLA highlighted the need for changes in the curriculum and changes in teaching style. Many of us had warned that it was crazy to compel children to stay on for an extra year until adequate provision was made to deal with the ROSLA group. The government pressed on regardless and the new rules came into effect in 1973.

Pupils who would by choice have left school at 15 were widely referred to as ROSLA pupils. The outcome was as much as we had expected. Only about 25% of them turned up for class in September.

During my 13-year teaching career, I learned that the boys in the D-streams, particularly the boys in their final year, reacted to the negative image everyone had of them in what became a self-fulfilling prophecy. I demonstrated that when they sensed a positive attitude on the part of the teacher and were given an opportunity to feel good about themselves, they were walking on air. I was able to show that the bad reputation was not always deserved. These were good lads who could work well if given the proper incentive.

I tried to provide teachers with an incentive to encourage the boys to work instead of resorting to punishment for not working. If the teacher respected the boys, the boys would respect him/her. Respect was the key to success.

I had quite a lot of success in changing the attitude of the boys to school and to schoolwork. I had little or no success in changing the attitude of the teachers. Some of the staff were convinced that I was teaching the boys bad habits and turning them off schoolwork. I was the reason they would no longer sit in the classroom and do menial tasks. I was giving them so many exciting things to do that they were no longer interested in doing the routine things which had to be practised and learned. These teachers could not bring themselves to believe that there was anything wrong with them or with their approach. It was the boys who were at fault, and me, of course.

At this time, we had our third principal. He was concerned that only 25% of the ROSLA pupils had turned up on the first day. He asked if I had any ideas. I said that it was clear to me that the school curriculum and teaching methods have a major role to play in non-attendance. It was essential that we made the curriculum meaningful for the ROSLA group.

The principal agreed. He said that first, we must get them into school to explain the new rules and tell them about the new curriculum. I suggested that I would run an intensive Community Service Week to encourage the boys to come to school. The school overlooked Our Lady's old people's home in Beechmount whose extensive grounds were overgrown and neglected. I said that the boys could cut the grass, trim the hedges and shrubs and dig over the flowerbeds.

Once we got the boys into school for the project, the principal and other senior staff could talk to them. They could explain that school attendance was now compulsory until the age of 16. They could outline what was on offer and advise that it would be both interesting and in their best interests to attend school.

The principal thought that helping Our Lady's old people's home was a great idea and agreed that it would provide an opportunity to talk to the boys and get them into class.

I sent a message to all the boys to explain that I had organised a Community Service Week for the first week in October, explaining what we would be doing. I expected a full turnout but wasn't expecting 110% attendance! I called the boys together to check and found that I had three boys I didn't recognise. At first, they wouldn't tell me their names but one of the St Peter's boys told me that they were friends of his from St Thomas's and asked, "Please can they stay? They will be no trouble, and they will work!" I said that I would have to let the principal in St Thomas's know they were with me. They could stay in the meantime. Later that day, I gave the names of the three boys to the principal of St Peter's, and he agreed to pass the message on.

I had full attendance all week and the boys did an excellent job. The Mother Superior was thrilled to have the grounds looking neat and tidy again and thanked the boys profusely for their work. The boys were pleased that their hard work had been appreciated.

Unfortunately, the full attendance I achieved that week did nothing to improve school attendance in the weeks that followed. Most of the boys did not turn up. Now the complaints started. I was like the Pied Piper. All I had to do was click my fingers and the boys came running. But it was easy for me. I was giving them what they wanted. Community Service should be reserved for those boys who worked hard in class. It should be organised at the end of the year as a reward for work well done. And it wasn't just the St Peter's staff who were complaining. The staff in St Thomas's were complaining also claiming that I was encouraging their pupils to miss school. None of the staff in St Thomas's made any attempt to contact their three students all week.

Chapter 14
Knowing When to Walk Away

The teachers could not, or would not, see that my success was not based on letting the boys do what they liked. There was no way they were 'just messing about outside'. I demanded high standards and would not accept shoddy work. If the work wasn't done properly, it had to be done again. I was always reminding them that 'if the job is worth doing, it is worth doing well'. If they didn't get it right the first time, they had an opportunity to do it again until they got it right.

We went out of our way to record the successes. Once the job was complete, it was there for all to see. There were no red biro marks scribbled all over it recording the failures. The boys had a sense of achievement and fulfilment. They felt they had shaken off the 'Dunce' label. School, on the other hand, had, for them, negative connotations. They didn't want to return to that.

I was starting to get a little tired of trying to convince the staff that it was time to look closely at the curriculum—particularly for the ROSLA group. I felt I had demonstrated that these were good lads who could work well if given the proper incentive. Unfortunately, many of the staff were still convinced that I was teaching them bad habits and turning them off schoolwork. I was giving them ideas above their station. They would no longer sit in the classroom and do routine classwork. There was nothing wrong with the teachers or the teaching. The problems lay with the boys and with me.

My 13 years of teaching raised several questions in my mind. I thought back on my own school days remembering how Master Sheeran had made education such fun. I couldn't wait to find out what was coming next, what new topics were to be learned, and new skills to be mastered. I just loved learning. Why can't we produce more children who are addicted to learning—children who love learning for its own sake rather than as a way to pass exams? Why do we make school so boring that many children leave vowing never to open another book?

The teachers would not accept that they would have to change their teaching style. The principal believed that I would have to change mine and he had a valid argument. He said the school wasn't insured for taking groups up the mountain. We would be in trouble if anyone got injured. We had no insurance for community service. What if someone got injured going to the shop, or using an axe to chop wood, or caused some damage in one of the houses? I had to agree that we should have insurance. I had no idea how much it would cost.

My colleagues on the staff seemed to have decided that I was head of security in the school as well as everything else. I got a message from one of the science teachers, 'There is a package in one of my cupboards which I didn't put there. Can you come and check it out?' Another teacher said to me, 'There are two men in the car park syphoning petrol out of my car. Can you go and talk to them?' I was extremely annoyed to receive such messages. I thought back on my altercation with the soldiers when they refused admission to one of the staff. I went to his aid, but no one came to mine. I can still see the line of teachers standing watching. No one made any attempt to intervene.

I was making no headway in trying to convince the staff that it was time to look closely at the curriculum—particularly for the ROSLA group. I had come to realise that the way forward was to sell my ideas to student teachers before they began their teaching careers and before they could develop bad habits. A vacancy in Trench House would provide me with the opportunity to get my ideas included in the teacher-training curriculum.

I began scanning the papers for vacant posts. I couldn't believe my luck. St Joseph's Teacher Training College was looking for a lecturer to take charge of youth and community work. It was a job made for me. St Joseph's was only a few minutes' walk from where I lived. The hours were more flexible than teaching—ideal in my situation in view of my wife's illness. Fortune smiled at me. I applied and was offered the post.

When I trained as a teacher, the focus was on learning teaching skills. Those of us who wished to teach in secondary schools followed a four-year course and were awarded a teacher's certificate. Despite the length of the course, degree status was not granted because the course was deemed by the universities to be too practical. While some of my colleagues resented not getting a degree, I didn't have any such concerns. In my view, the course needed to be practical. We needed to learn how to teach.

In 1968, the Senate of Queen's University granted St Mary's and St Joseph's recognition for the instruction of matriculated students of the university in courses leading to the degree of bachelor of education. The university agreed to award degree status on condition that there was more emphasis on academic achievement. Later this was extended to offer students the opportunity to be awarded an honours degree. The bias was tilting more and more towards academic achievement as students selected a main subject and a subsidiary subject. This meant that a student could graduate with a first-class honours degree in his/her main subject without having reached a first-class level in teaching. Perhaps even more worrying was the fact that they could have a first-class honours degree while being exceptionally weak at English and Maths. I didn't think this was good for someone who wanted to teach. Teaching skills were no longer the main priority. How could young teachers make lessons interesting for pupils in the classroom?

Teaching the 'A'-streams might not present too much of a problem but how would they manage the 'D'-streams where the pupils didn't really want to learn? In my opinion, this change of emphasis played a large part in the growing problem of indiscipline in schools.

My course would focus on working with disaffected young people. Teaching skills would be the main priority. As time passed, a growing number of newly qualified teachers would welcome the challenge of working with the D-streams and helping the young people be the best they could be.

Chapter 15
Any Irishman Will Do

The teachers in St Peter's complained that all I had to do was to click my fingers and the boys came running because I always gave them what they wanted. The truth was that the older boys were not interested in any school-related activities. Most of the D-stream boys had been looking forward to leaving school when they were 14 (or thereabouts) because that was how it was before St Peter's opened. If I could get them to listen to me, I could tell them my plans to make schoolwork interesting. If I achieved that, I was able to win most of them over. But there were always a few difficult nuts to crack.

I recall one boy, Gerry, who never really got involved in anything. He was always watching me but would never look me in the eye. He seemed evasive, shifty-eyed and vague. Most people consider that as a sign of dishonesty. However, there is another possibility. I believe that such furtive eye movements can have evolutionary roots in the prime instincts of animals, including human beings, to continually survey the surrounding landscape for food or danger. I wondered if he suffered abuse at home and was always looking for an escape route. He never let me get close enough to him for me to find out.

Then I heard rumours that Gerry had a reputation for stealing and shoplifting. I was told that he was abusing alcohol and drugs. He stopped coming to school and I lost all contact with him.

I left St Peter's at the end of June 1974, to take up my new job in St Joseph's Training College where I would be training teachers. A few months later, on 21 November 1974, I heard that bombs had gone off in the Mulberry Bush and the Tavern in the Town, two pubs in the centre of Birmingham, killing 21 people and injuring 182, the worst of many attacks in England in a sustained campaign by the IRA. I was surprised to read that the police had arrested the suspects and charged them with the offence. I assumed that the police had been watching the suspects when they were so quick off the mark. But when I read that they had arrested six Irishmen, I wondered. Had they been told to arrest someone quickly to calm the local populace? Was it a case of 'Any Irishman will do?'

The six co-defendants were ready-made to tie to the bombings because they knew each other, they were all Irish, they were all from Northern Ireland, and they were all living in Birmingham. They were arrested within hours of the bombings. The police said that the evidence against them fell into three categories: *association with the IRA; forensic tests; the confessions.*

No witnesses placed any of the men at the scene of the bombings or established a link between them and the IRA. Searches of their homes, vehicles and belongings didn't produce any bomb-making material or any evidence indicating they had been involved in the bombings or that they were associated with the IRA. Consequently, the primary 'evidence' against the six was reduced to two: forensic evidence and the confessions.

Forensic evidence was crucial. Home Office forensic scientist Dr Frank Skuse told the jury that he had used the Griess test[22] to check if any of the six defendants had handled explosives. Timing is critical with this test. The test should be carried out as soon after the alleged offence as possible; co-defendants should all be tested at the same time; there should be no lengthy delays between tests. However, there was confusion over the time Dr Skuse ran the test, or indeed how many times he had run the test. He could not explain lengthy intervals between tests. His evidence seemed to suggest that he had run the test three times. He denied that one of the tests gave negative results for all the defendants. He kept no contemporaneous note of the times at which he carried out the tests. Indeed, he kept very few notes of any kind. He did not even record the chemical formula he had used, despite knowing that the strength of the chemical used is critical—too strong or too weak could invalidate the test.

As a Home Office forensic scientist investigating the bombings and giving evidence for the Crown at the trial, Dr Skuse failed to show the skill, knowledge, care and thoroughness to be expected of him in that role. Nonetheless,

---

[22] The Griess test is an analytical chemistry test which detects the presence of nitrite ion in solution. The test has also been widely used for the detection of nitrates, which are a common component of explosives. However, the solvent Skuse had used in the test for nitroglycerine, 1 per cent caustic soda, would also have produced a positive result if the men had handled nitrocellulose.

he told the jury that the test showed with 99% certainty that two of the defendants had handled explosives.

Dr Hugh Kenneth Black of the Royal Institute of Chemistry and formerly HM Chief Inspector of Explosives for the Home Office told the court that it is an accepted principle in science that there are no certainties, only probabilities. If one of the tests returned negative results that should raise doubts over all the tests. He said that he had personally tested all the defendants and that all his tests had shown negative results. He asked whether Dr Skuse had considered the possibility of an innocent explanation for the positive result.

Dr Skuse replied that no substance other than nitro-glycerine could have given him the positive results. He said he was ***absolutely certain*** that two of the six defendants had handled explosives.

The judge dismissed Dr Black's concerns, ignored his long experience and expertise and accepted Dr Skuse's 'absolute certainty'—despite the shortcomings I have listed above.

It seemed that Dr Frank Skuse liaised with Detective Chief Superintendent George Reade regarding the evidence against the accused, something he was not permitted to do. Reade appeared to be the first to learn that Skuse would announce with absolute certainty that two of the six accused had handled explosives. This was the green light he had been waiting for. He and his specialist interrogation team set about acquiring the 'confessions'.

While the men were in the custody of the West Midlands Police, they were allegedly deprived of food and sleep and were sometimes interrogated for as much as 12 hours without a break. Threats were made against them and their families. They were beaten, threatened that police dogs would be let loose on them, and threatened with mock executions. Four signed confessions. All were remanded to HM Prison Winson Green.

The confessions were all very short, with little information about the planting of the bombs. There was no mention in any of the confessions about who made the bombs, where they were made, or how and where the bombs were primed. There was disagreement regarding the number of bombs planted and about who did the planning. All the 'confessions' referred to the bombs being in white plastic bags. However, the forensic scientists who sifted through the wreckage of the pubs later told the jury that each bomb had been in a small suitcase or holdall.

Taking into consideration the questions raised above together with the fact that all the defendants showed signs of physical abuse when they appeared in court, one might expect that the judge would have concerns about the confessions. If he had, he kept those concerns to himself. The jury found the six men guilty of murder and each received 21 life sentences.

The six maintained their innocence and insisted police had coerced them into signing false confessions through severe physical and psychological abuse. Their first appeal, in March 1976 was heard by the Lord Chief Justice, Lord Widgery[23],

---

[23] Lord Widgery was not a friend of the Irish.
The Widgery Report on Bloody Sunday: an inquiry into the events of 30 January 1972 in Derry where soldiers of the Parachute Regiment shot and killed 13 unarmed civil rights marchers (a 14th person died shortly afterwards). Widgery heard testimony from the

Lord Lawton and Mr Justice Thompson. In dismissing the appeal Lord Widgery concluded, there was no evidence that they had been beaten 'beyond the ordinary'.

In June 1976, Judge Swanwick acquitted 14 prison officers of assaulting the six at Winson Green Prison. He claimed the men had made lying accusations against the police at Lancaster [the venue for the 1975 trial] in order to try and wriggle out of their true confessions. He did not say who beat the men, although it was accepted that they had been beaten.

In November 1977, the six sued for injuries inflicted by the police at Morecambe and New Street, Birmingham. In January 1980, the Master of the Rolls, Lord Denning upheld a police appeal for the action to be struck out as an abuse of process. Justifying his decision, he said, "If the six men win, it will mean that the police were guilty of perjury, that they were guilty of violence and threats, and the convictions were erroneous…This is such an appalling vista that every person in the land would say it cannot be right that these actions should go any further."

"If the six had been hanged," Lord Denning later remarked, "we shouldn't have all these campaigns to get them released."

In January 1987, Douglas Hurd, the Home Secretary, referred the case back to the Court of Appeal and ordered a

---

soldiers, who claimed they had been shot at, while the marchers insisted that no one from the march was armed. Widgery's report, published in April 1972 took the side of the soldiers. Widgery put the main blame for the deaths on the march organisers for creating a dangerous situation where a confrontation was inevitable.

new inquiry by the Devon and Cornwall police after Granada TV's 'World in Action' questioned the reliability of the forensic evidence.

In January 1988, the appeal was dismissed by the Lord Chief Justice, Lord Lane, who said, "The longer this hearing has gone on the more convinced this court has become that the verdict of the jury [in the 1975 trial] was correct."

In April 1988, the six were refused leave to appeal to the House of Lords. Lord Denning said, "It is better that some innocent men remain in gaol than the integrity of the English judicial system should be impugned."

At every stage of the Birmingham Six case, the state has concerned itself with keeping the lid on its Pandora's box[24]. Each time new evidence came forward to discredit the original judgement, the source and/or the witnesses were ridiculed and defamed.

The Birmingham Six story is not only one of extreme police misconduct. The actions of some of the judiciary, who seemed more concerned with upholding the reputation of the criminal justice system than seeking the truth, took it to an additional level of concern.

I believe that the judges in the trial and in the various appeals were convinced that the Birmingham Six were innocent. The only reason their appeals were turned down was that if they had been upheld police, prison officers, government officials and members of the judiciary at a very high level, would have been brought into disrepute.

---

[24] Any source of great and unexpected trouble. (From Greek Mythology)

But the growing evidence of innocence became irresistible. The six were allowed a second full appeal in 1991. There was new evidence of police fabrication and suppression of evidence, question marks over how the 'confessions' were obtained and question marks over the forensic evidence which had been accepted by the court. The convictions were declared both unsafe and unsatisfactory and quashed by the Court of Appeal on 14 March 1991. The Birmingham Six spent 16 years in prison for a crime of which they were entirely innocent.

The collapse of the case against the Birmingham Six exposed the enormity of the cover-up over which 11 judges had presided. Without them, the intricate web of lies and deception woven by prison officers and police officers, including former Detective Chief Superintendent George Reade, could not have withstood the repeated challenges of the Birmingham Six and their solicitors.

I decided to look again at two other recent IRA bombings—the Guildford pub bombing of 5 October 1974, and the Woolwich pub bombing of 7 November 1974. Again, the police appeared to have been very much on the ball. The suspects were arrested in record time and remanded in custody. They were Paul Hill, Gerry Conlon, Patrick Armstrong and Carole Richardson—three Irish men and one English woman. They became known as the 'Guildford Four'.

I was surprised when I saw the names. Gerry Conlon had been a pupil of mine when I was teaching in St Peter's Secondary School in Belfast. This was the pupil I was told was into shoplifting and stealing to provide money for drink and drugs. I found it hard to believe that the IRA would have asked him to be a member of their bombing team.

The Guildford Four confessed to the bombing after intense interrogation by the police. These confessions were later retracted but remained the basis of the case against them. They would later be alleged to be the result of coercion by the police, ranging from intimidation to torture—including threats against family members.

The judge took no cognisance of the defence claim that the Guildford Four did not 'fit the bill' of IRA involvement because of the way they lived. Gerry asserted that the IRA would not have used him due to his record of shoplifting and petty crime. He pointed out that he had been expelled from Fianna Éireann (the junior IRA) because of his crimes. Two of the others lived in a squat and were also involved with drugs and petty crime.

Justice Lord John Donaldson who presided over the Guildford Four trial and over the Maguire Seven trial (see below), expressed regret that the four had not been charged with high treason, which still had a mandatory death penalty. Although no hangings had been carried out in the UK since 1964, treason still carried the death penalty until 1998. The Guildford Four were found guilty of the Guildford pub bombings of 5 October 1974, and the Woolwich pub bombing of 7 November 1974. They were all sentenced to life in prison.

On 3 December 1974, Anne Maguire was washing up after the evening meal in her house in Kilburn, North London. With her was her six-year-old daughter, Anne-Marie, her husband and her second oldest son, John. Also in the house were her brother Shaun Smyth, her brother-in-law, Giuseppe Conlon and a family friend Pat O'Neill. Pat's wife had been admitted to hospital that afternoon and he had called to ask

Anne if she would look after his children so that he could go and visit his wife.

Anne's other children, Vincent and Patrick Jr, were out. Vincent was attending classes at college as a trainee gas engineer and Patrick was at the local youth club. Giuseppe had arrived in London that day having travelled from Belfast in order to speak to the solicitors representing his son Gerry Conlon.

Suddenly officers from the Surrey Constabulary crashed through the doorway. They had dogs with them and were armed. Pandemonium broke out. The family would later learn that Gerry Conlon and Paul Hill had told the police in their false confessions that Conlon's aunt, Anne Maguire, had taught them how to make bombs.

When Vincent and Patrick Jr returned home, they were arrested along with the rest of the household. Despite extensive searches, no incriminating evidence was found. Nonetheless, they were all told that they were being arrested for terrorist offences. They were split up and taken to two North London police stations. Each of them had their hands swabbed and scrapings were taken from under their fingernails. The forensic scientists told the police that the tests were positive for nitro-glycerine. Anne and her husband Patrick, Vincent and Patrick Jr, Sean Smyth, Guiseppe Conlon and Pat O'Neill were all charged with possession of nitro-glycerine which, it was alleged, they passed to the IRA to make bombs. They became known as the Maguire Seven.

Evidence before the court claimed that traces of nitro-glycerine were found on the hands of Anne and Patrick Maguire. They were each sentenced to 14 years in prison. The other three adults were sentenced to 12 years each in prison.

The older of the two juveniles received a five-year sentence and the youngest was sentenced to four years.

In 1989, detectives from Avon and Somerset Constabulary, investigating how Surrey Police dealt with the Guildford Four case, found a high level of duplicity in relation to Surrey Police's handling of the four and their statements. Typed notes from police interviews had been extensively edited. Deletions and additions had been made and the notes had been rearranged. The notes and their amendments were consistent with hand-written and typed notes presented at the trial, which suggested that the hand-written notes were made after the interviews had been conducted. The notes presented had been described in court as contemporaneous records. Manuscript notes relating to an interview with one of the defendants showed that a fifth statement was taken in breach of Judges' Rules[25] and may well have been inadmissible as evidence. This information was not made available to the Department of Public Prosecutions (DPP) or the defence and

---

[25] The Judges Rules are a Code of Best Practice when questioning suspects.

The Rules:

allowed the police to question any person with a view to finding out whether, or by whom, an offence had been committed,

required the police to give a caution when they had evidence to suspect that a person had committed an offence,

required a further caution when a person was charged and prohibited questioning after charging save in exceptional circumstances,

required a record of questioning to be kept,

gave guidance on the best way to record a formal written statement. The rules also included administrative guidance on access to defence counsel, and on questioning children and foreigners.

the officers involved had denied under oath that such an interview had happened. Detention records were inconsistent with the times and durations of the claimed interviews, as reported by the Surrey police.

The Lord Chief Justice, Lord Lane, concluded that regardless of the impact of the content of the material discovered by Avon and Somerset Police, or the alibis or additional evidence the appellants wished to introduce, the level of duplicity meant that all the police evidence was suspect, and the case for the prosecution was unsafe.

Both groups' convictions were eventually declared 'unsafe and unsatisfactory' and reversed in 1989 and 1991, respectively, after they had served lengthy prison sentences for crimes of which they were totally innocent.

In October 1989, the UK government appointed Appeal Court Justice Sir John May to undertake a judicial inquiry into the suspect convictions of the Guildford Four and the Maguire Seven. The findings of the inquiry criticised the trial judge Lord Donaldson of Lymington. It unearthed improprieties in the handling of scientific evidence that were relevant to the other cases. Three police officers were charged with conspiracy to pervert the course of justice in the wake of the inquiry but found not guilty in 1993.

Over 700 documents, including secret testimony, were collected by Justice Sir John May's inquiry and were due to be unsealed for public access in the National Archives on 1 January 2020. However, on 31 December 2019, the Home Office removed all 700 records from the National Archive and took them back into government control just one day before they were to be opened to the public. The files remain sealed.

The government's action tells us all we need to know about Justice Sir John May's report. Remembering Lord Denning's words when he threw out a civil action that the Birmingham Six had brought against West Midlands Police in 1980, I imagine that his comment on the report would be something like the following:

'The report presents such an appalling vista of police perjury and violence, and of misconduct on the part of senior members of the judiciary and some government officials, that it cannot be right that it be released into the public domain[26]'.

None of the key figures in the British legal and criminal justice establishment who were responsible for the wrongful prosecution of the Birmingham Six, the Guildford Four and the Maguire Seven were formally held accountable for their role in the scandal.

Sir Norman John Skelhorn, KBE, QC, an English barrister, was Director of Public Prosecutions for England and Wales from 1964 to 1977. In 1973, he became entangled in a row that erupted around the use of torture in Northern Ireland. Edward Heath, who was Prime Minister from 19 June 1970 to 4 March 1974, had banned sensory deprivation in light of the report by Sir Edmund Compton into internment and interrogation techniques used by the British army and the Royal Ulster Constabulary. In October 1973, while being questioned at a meeting of the Harvard Law School Forum, Sir Norman did not deny that torture had taken place. On the

---

[26] This is not what Lord Denning said. I don't know if he said anything about Sir John May's report. But my guess is that he would comment on the report. I would guess that he would say something like what I have written.

contrary, he stated that when dealing with 'Irish terrorists', any methods were justified. He oversaw the Crown's prosecution of the Guildford Four and the Maguire Seven, as well as the prosecution of the Birmingham Six. Clearly, the same rules applied. He retired as DPP in 1977 before a critical report by Lord Devlin, recommending statutory prosecution safeguards, was published.

Dr Skuse joined the Home Office forensic science service in 1963 at the age of 28. After six years of service, he was promoted in 1969 to the next grade of principal scientific officer. His career was uneventful until the early 1980s, when his managers noted some falling off in his performance. A decision was taken to review all the available records at the laboratory. These covered Dr Skuse's written evidence in some 350 cases, dating back not just to 1975, but to 1966. No evidence was found that Dr Skuse had misreported facts, had been biased in his reports, or had been negligent in his work. There were no grounds for suspecting that Dr Skuse's work had led to any miscarriage of justice.

However, deterioration in performance was noted in a number of staff reports in the early 1980s. Consequently, Dr Skuse was informed that the department was making moves to secure his compulsory retirement on the grounds of limited efficiency. He agreed to take voluntary retirement on 31 October 1985, at the tender age of 51. The department had gone to a lot of effort attempting to demonstrate that there was no connection between Dr Skuse's retirement and the case of the Birmingham bombings!

Otherwise, while these three trials put the spotlight on extreme police misconduct and raised questions over the actions of some of the judiciary, this was no barrier to promotion. Indeed, as far as I could ascertain, all the key British figures involved in these wrongful convictions were subsequently promoted and reached the top of their respective legal or policing professions.

Gerry, my former pupil, with the assistance of another former St Peter's boy, Richard O'Rawe, wrote an autobiography *Proved Innocent* which was adapted into the film 'In the Name of the Father'. He was suffering from cancer and died at home in Belfast on 21 June 2014, aged 60.

His father was also wrongly convicted as one of the 'Maguire Seven'. He was arrested when he travelled to London to get legal advice for his son. He had a chronic lung ailment and died in prison in 1980.

The youngest member of the Maguire Seven also wrote a book entitled:

My Father's Watch: The Story of a Child Prisoner in 70s Britain which was released in May 2008.

Chapter 16
33 Years As a Lay Magistrate

I was a frequent visitor to Belfast Juvenile Court. As part of their training on teaching disaffected young people, I brought my students to the court to find out how young people who get themselves on the wrong side of the law are dealt with. I accepted an invitation from the Resident Magistrate (RM) in Belfast Juvenile Court, to 'join us on this side of the Bench'. He said that I would have a better understanding of how the system worked.

I was appointed a Lay Magistrate in April 1976. Appointees were referred to as *Lay Panel Members*, at that time. However, to avoid confusion, I will use the term *Lay Magistrate* which is the official title since *The Justice (NI) Act 2002* was implemented in 2005.

In those days, a candidate's name was submitted to the Lord Chancellor's *Lay Panel Advisory Committee*. Membership of that committee was kept secret from the public. If a nominee was rejected, there was no way of finding out why. Clearly, it was necessary to have the right contacts to guarantee an appointment. The names of those appointed as Lay Magistrates were not made known publicly either.

It was purely coincidental that the Lynn Committee Report (*The Protection and Welfare of the Young and the Treatment of Young Offenders*) which recommended that two lay persons should sit with the resident magistrate in cases involving juveniles, was published in 1938, the year I was born. The recommendation became law in the *Children (Juvenile Courts) Act (Northern Ireland) 1942*. I never even dreamt of being one of those *laypersons*. There was no way I would ever have been appointed if I had not got to know the RM through bringing students to the court.

There was justification for the secrecy because we were at the height of *The Troubles,* and judges were regarded as 'legitimate targets' by the IRA. Several judges were murdered. An RM who lived next door to me was warned by the police that he was on an IRA hit list. He, and one of his colleagues, left Northern Ireland and took up posts in Hong Kong.

No one had been attacked simply because he/she was a Lay Magistrate, but that could change at any time. It was better to be safe than sorry since Lay Magistrates fulfil a judicial role. I always warned my son Liam not to mention to his friends that his dad was a magistrate in the courts. That is not to say that I believed the IRA didn't know. I thought they probably did, especially since I had also been appointed as a Justice of the Peace (JP). I was the only JP in Catholic West Belfast.

Some years after my appointments as a Lay Magistrate and a Justice of the Peace (1976), I was visiting my brother in Great Yarmouth. My nephew, Paul, informed me that his friend, who was in the army, had just completed a tour of duty in West Belfast. His friend wanted to know whether Paul had any relatives living there. Paul said that he had an uncle living there. His friend then told him that all patrols in the Andersonstown area had been informed that a Dr McCarney who lived in Andersonstown might be subject to attack by Republican elements in the community because he was a Justice of the Peace and a Lay Magistrate. Patrols should be aware that he might need protection.

My work, as a Lay Magistrate, was mainly with troublesome young people, and they got in everybody's hair. So, the IRA was not too concerned that I was trying to sort them out. The police thoughtfully never asked me to hold a special court to order the remand in custody of suspected IRA men who had just been arrested.

My suspicion that the IRA probably knew all about my activities was confirmed when two Sinn Fein councillors (Belfast City Council) arrived at my door asking me to sign their election returns. Councillors had to have their election expenses checked by a JP who would confirm that they had kept within the prescribed limit. On many occasions, people called at my door asking for a variety of forms to be signed. The strangest was being asked to sign a form to have the body of the applicant's mother released from the morgue! It was more usual to be asked to confirm the identity of someone whose parent had just died in a nursing home so that they could collect whatever small amount of money and valuables had been left or collect an insurance policy. Of course, there was the signing of everyday forms like passport applications. So, people were aware of my roles but saw me as someone who was willing to help when they were in difficulties.

However, people in general would not have been aware of the wide range of duties of lay magistrates. These included:

- sitting with a district judge in youth courts hearing cases in criminal matters involving children aged 10 to 18.
- sitting with a district judge in family proceedings courts dealing with civil issues relating to the welfare, care, protection, and custody of children aged 0 to 18.
- sitting with a county court judge as an assessor in appeals from youth courts.
- dealing with certain ex-parte applications[27], such as emergency protection orders or recovery orders.
- presiding in special courts where a person is brought before a court for the first time, and
- hearing complaints with a view to issuing summonses and warrants.

As a result of the Good Friday Agreement in 1998, the appointment of Lay Magistrates is now totally transparent. A major recruitment campaign to attract 300 people to become Lay Magistrates was launched in May 2004. Applications were encouraged from all sections of society in Northern Ireland. The campaign was advertised in the local press. Lay Magistrates were appointed strictly on merit in line with competence-based selection criteria. The appointment process encompassed the principles of equal opportunities and equality. The new Lay Magistrates underwent a comprehensive training programme and took up their new roles in April 2005.

---

[27] An application to the court by one party where the other party is not present and not represented.

Lay Magistrates were unpaid during most of my time on the Bench and sat on average one day per month. The payment was recommended by the Criminal Justice Review, following the Good Friday Agreement, in order to open the door to working-class people who could not otherwise afford to participate. The only reason I could afford to sit was that I was always able to rearrange my lecturing schedule for the days when I was called to court. The students were always very cooperative in agreeing to reschedule lectures once per month. The college authorities had no objections so long as I got my work done.

A system of payment was introduced in April 2005—£160 per day or £80 per half day. Having worked for 30 years purely in a voluntary capacity, I was not happy with the idea of being paid for the work I did in the courts. I did not believe that payment would enhance the quality of justice. But I am beginning to run ahead of myself. Let me get back to 1976.

I will deal first with those incidents where I sat alone:

- presiding in special courts where a person is brought before a court for the first time, and
- hearing complaints with a view to issuing summonses and warrants.

I mentioned above that the police did not ask me to preside at a special court where IRA suspects had been arrested. I believe they were acting in my best interests because of my exposed situation. However, I regularly held special courts to deal with requests from social services to have a child taken into care. Quite often these requests came late at night, sometimes in the early hours of the morning when a child was deemed to be in such danger that the hearing could not be postponed until the next normal court sitting. I would first receive a phone call asking whether I was available to hear the case and then would be given a brief outline of what was involved. Sometime later, one or more social workers would arrive at my door accompanied by a solicitor.

I always took these cases very seriously because I believed that, if a child (or children) was to be taken away from his/her parents, it needed to be very clear that the child would be in grave danger otherwise. This was particularly important since the parent was not represented at this hearing. So, I would consider all the evidence in detail and then hear from the solicitor. This could take anything from 30 minutes to 2 hours—and remember, this might well be in the middle of the night. I would then give my response. It was necessary to be well acquainted with the law to avoid mistakes. I could order the social workers to appear in court the next morning for a full hearing (where the parent would be represented) or allow up to seven days to enable social services to complete their investigations.

The cases were usually straightforward but sometimes were quite complicated. Once I was asked to make a care order for a child who had not yet been born. The social worker presented compelling evidence that the child, once born, would be in grave danger. I said that I couldn't make an order if there was no child. So, we sat drinking tea until we received a phone call from the Mater Hospital around 1 am that the child had been safely delivered.

There were often complicated issues to be considered like whether I had jurisdiction to hear the case. If the child lived outside the boundary of the Belfast court, I could not deal with it. Once I had a case of a child from Limerick whose parents were seriously abusing hard drugs. The child was being neglected and the grandfather had taken it to Belfast. The parents had arrived to reclaim their child. What was to be done? Or the case of a child found in the company of an adult at Belfast docks—both of African origin. The adult was arrested on suspicion of being an illegal immigrant. She claimed the child was her daughter but didn't know the child's name. Or a request to issue an order to have a child detained under the Mental Health Act. The Act is quite clear that two doctors, at least one of whom is a psychiatrist, must give evidence that detention is in the best interests of the child. The social worker gives evidence that there is imminent danger of serious injury to the child him/herself or to others. Could I issue a temporary, holding order?

I also sat alone while hearing complaints with a view to issuing summonses and warrants. These were almost always in the early hours of the morning. In these cases, I would be dealing with the police and not with social workers. Again, I took these cases very seriously. I would not sign a warrant simply because a police officer said he/she had evidence to back it up. I always insisted that they come into the house, sit down, and present the evidence in detail. If they could convince me that they had good grounds, then I would sign the warrant. In later years, drugs became a major issue, usually handling or selling hard drugs. I was always amazed at how many respectable people were growing cannabis in their own homes.

Sometimes even the police would get things wrong, as they were not always totally au fait with the legislation. It was always necessary to be on one's toes and to have the reference books handy—just in case. It was much more critical to be careful while sitting alone. Things were different in court where the resident magistrate would, generally, know the legislation inside out.

In 1976, the first-tier professional judges were called *Resident Magistrates*, or simply *RMs*. Following the Good Friday Agreement and the Criminal Justice Review, they were renamed *District Judges* so that there would be no confusion in the minds of the public between *Resident Magistrates* and *Lay Magistrates*.

Judges sit alone in our adult courts. When dealing with children, they sit as a *Bench* of three. The *Bench* is made up of one full-time professional judge (*RM* or *district judge*) and two part-time judges (*Lay Magistrates*). One of the part-time judges must be a woman.

While there should be three judges on the Bench in the juvenile court, it is permissible for the court to sit with the RM/district judge and one lay judge if the second lay judge has been notified but fails to turn up. (Should both lay judges, for whatever reason, fail to turn up the RM/district judge could sit alone—although this would be highly unusual).

All three members of the Bench have equal authority. Consequently, if there is disagreement about a finding of guilt, or about what to do with the child, it is possible for the part-time judges to outvote their full-time professional colleague. However, this would be a rare occurrence. If there was a disagreement, we would retire and discuss the pros and cons. We would always aim for consensus. During my thirty-three years on the Bench, I can only recall two or three occasions when we outvoted the full-time professional judge.

I never had any disagreements with the RM who appointed me. He always treated his lay colleagues with the utmost respect and always worked for consensus. He extended the same level of respect to the defendants, and to their families, always listening to what they had to say and making sure they understood the thinking behind the court's decision.

I remember once we had a defendant from Derry who had been remanded in custody to St Patrick's Training School (in Belfast). His trial had to be postponed on three separate occasions because his solicitor, who was also from Derry, failed to turn up. The defendant did not want the case adjourned. However, the charges were serious and there was a good possibility that he would receive a custodial sentence. In these circumstances, the court could not proceed until the child was represented. I was sitting on the fourth occasion when the case was set for hearing. True to form, the solicitor failed to show up and the case was adjourned yet again. The defendant exploded and called us for all the names of the day. He told us that his father was one of the few lucky ones in Derry as he was in full-time employment. Each time the case was set for trial, he had to take a day off work. This was the fourth day he had taken off for nothing. Could we not see he was going to lose his job? The boy could have been charged with contempt of court for his abusive language.

Instead, the RM allowed him to continue until he calmed down. He explained that we were not allowed to hear the case until the defendant's solicitor was present. He then said, "I'm not supposed to advise you in these matters but maybe you should consider changing your solicitor."

Once we were hearing an application from social services to have children taken into care. The social workers didn't believe that the mother was a bad mother. They accepted that she loved her children. The problem was that she simply couldn't cope. She herself was concerned that she wasn't providing for her children the way she would like to. So, when Family Allowance Day arrived, she would have a party for them with lots of cake and fizzy drinks. Most of the Family Allowance money would go to the party. Consequently, she wouldn't have enough money to see her through the week. The children would go hungry until the next party day. Social services today would put a mother's helper into the house to teach the mother how to budget her money and make sure the children had sufficient food every day. She would never become a financial expert, but the aim would be to get her to the level of 'good enough' parenting so that the children could stay at home with her.

Social services had a different way of thinking in the 1980s. They just took the children into care. We were reluctant to take the children from a mother who clearly loved them, but they were being neglected. Our hands were tied. We made a care order. The mother was clearly very distressed. The RM tried to explain to her why we had no option. He added that when she got herself organised and was able to provide a warm, welcoming home, she could come back to the court, and we would have her children returned to her. She looked at him and said, "How can I do that when you have just torn my home and my family apart?"

I recall another case where social services were also asking for a care order, and we were certainly going to grant it. There were three children involved—two boys aged 13 and

15 and a girl of 12. The evidence presented was that the mother had taught the boys how to have sex with their sister. The mother had allegedly held the girl down while the boys had intercourse with her. Then, when the older boy was sufficiently proficient, she allowed him to have sex with her. I was horrified. I was aware that fathers sometimes sexually abused their children, but this was the first time I had come across a mother being involved in such horrific abuse. We made the care order, and the RM instructed the prosecutor to check that the mother was being suitably dealt with in the adult court.

Another sex abuse case was more problematic. A 14-year-old boy was accused of molesting a five-year-old girl. From the evidence presented, it was unclear whether he had done anything more than look to see how girls were different from boys. The case was complicated by the fact that the boy had Down's Syndrome. We called in a paediatrician for advice. Her assessment was that the boy's IQ was that of a child aged five or six. The doctor advised that it was not unusual for children of five or six to wonder how girls and boys differed and to want to have a look. From talking to the girl, the doctor was convinced that she had removed her own pants and had allowed the boy to look. The girl's evidence was that nothing had happened apart from looking. We gave the boy a conditional discharge—the condition being that his parents arrange counselling for him.

Some RMs resented having to sit with Lay Magistrates and would have been happier working alone. They particularly resented the fact that the Lay Magistrates could outvote them and force the RM to accept a majority decision if they didn't agree with his/her recommendation.

One of these occasions was the case of a child charged with riotous behaviour—specifically with throwing a brick at a soldier. My two colleagues decided that he was guilty and should receive a custodial sentence. I argued that we could not make a finding of guilt because the soldier was clearly telling lies. The other two were appalled that I would even suggest that a member of the security forces would tell lies in court. I had taken careful note of the evidence presented in court and went back over it with them. The rioting took place in the Short Strand, in East Belfast. The streetlights were out, and the place was in darkness. More than 100 young people took part in the rioting. The soldier said the defendant had thrown a brick at him. When asked if the brick had hit him, he replied that it had not as the defendant was 'out of range'.

When asked how he could be sure that it was the defendant who had thrown the brick, he claimed that he could see him clearly. When he was reminded that he had said earlier that the place was in darkness, he replied that the defendant was only a couple of feet away from him. My Lay Magistrate colleague agreed that the soldier's evidence was unreliable. The RM insisted that the defendant had clearly been involved in the rioting and that we must find him guilty. I reminded the RM that the defendant was charged with throwing a brick at a particular soldier and that we could not accept that the charge had been proven 'beyond a reasonable doubt'. The RM was most annoyed and when we went back into the court, he announced that we had decided against his advice that the case be dismissed. I was concerned that the RM's bias was showing.

Sometimes the RMs appeared to believe that, because we were *Lay Magistrates*, we knew nothing about the law. A young man from Ballymurphy was charged with throwing a petrol bomb at the police. On this occasion, the evidence was quite clear, and the defendant agreed that he was 'guilty as charged'. We then disagreed as to what our 'disposition' should be, i.e., how we should dispose of the case. The RM insisted that we must give him a long custodial sentence. I pointed out that the police involved had spoken in the boy's defence. They told the court that they had placed the boy on curfew and ordered him to report to the police station daily. They said that the boy and his family had cooperated fully with them—an unusual occurrence in Ballymurphy. They informed us that the defendant had never come to their attention before and that he was due to sit his GCSEs in a few weeks. They would be happy with a conditional discharge. The RM informed us that our hands were tied.

The legislation said we must impose a custodial sentence for throwing a petrol bomb. I asked him to show us where in the legislation it said that. He then said it didn't say that we must impose a custodial sentence but, clearly, we should impose a custodial sentence since the offence was a serious one. My counterargument was that the police officers who had been attacked believed that the defendant's action had been totally out of character, and they were prepared to give him another chance. We should do the same. The RM would not agree. When we returned to the court, he announced that we had decided by majority vote to give the defendant a conditional discharge.

My powers of persuasion were more fruitful in a case arising from the death of hunger striker Bobby Sands (5 May 1981). Tensions were high following the lengthy hunger strike. West Belfast erupted when news came through that

Bobby Sands had died. There were many arrests and some of those arrested were children—young people under the age of 18—who were brought before the Juvenile Court. There was no argument about whether they had been rioting. The defendants told the court that they had been in bed and had been awakened by the sound of car horns, bin lids and people shouting. They had gone out to investigate and had got caught up in the rioting. The question for us was what the penalty should be. My two colleagues thought we should come down hard. The defendants should have stayed in bed. There was no reason for them to go out and get involved in rioting. We should teach them a lesson and send the message out that anyone involved in rioting would be dealt with harshly.

I said it was all very well for people not living in West Belfast. I, too, had been sound asleep in bed and had been awakened by the din. I, too, had got up and could only guess what had happened. If I had been a teenager, I would probably have gone out to investigate. Instead, I went into the kitchen and made a pot of tea for myself and my wife. We sat all night drinking tea and listening to the rioting. The situation was exceptional. We should take that into account. I suggested that we impose conditional discharges. Then, if the defendants appeared back in court within the next twelve months, they could be penalised for both the current offence and for any new offences. My colleagues agreed.

As the urban guerrilla war intensified, I was concerned that the boys in the school were getting involved. And yet there were only three occasions when pupils or former pupils appeared before me. If I recognised a pupil or former pupil in a case which we were about to hear, I would have to 'Declare an Interest' and withdraw.

In the first case, a former pupil was charged with being in possession of a rifle. He was stopped by soldiers in Belfast city centre and found to have a rifle under his overcoat. When a soldier tried to take the rifle, he held onto it and refused to let it go. He started screaming that he had found the rifle and that he wanted to get the reward. He insisted that he was on his way to the police station, which was only a couple of streets away, to hand the gun in and get his reward. He created such a row that a passing police patrol stopped. The soldiers explained what had happened and said they thought the young man was crazy. They were happy to hand him over to the police. He was released on police bail.

A police officer appeared in court and outlined the story as above. He said they had assessed the boy as having a very low IQ and they had decided not to press charges. I knew the boy and would have agreed that he had a low IQ. However, he wasn't stupid. He was caught in possession of a rifle but had managed to avoid being charged with any offence.

The second case was similar. The defendant was a former pupil of the school, although I had never taught him as he was in the B-stream. I asked him one time about his older brother, John, who was a first-class athlete. He replied that John was the black sheep of their family. I asked him why. He said, "Because he is the only one in the family who refused to join the IRA."

I told the RM that I would have to withdraw from this case. He replied, "Let's hear what the charge is first." We went out and took our seats. As we sat down, the defendant winked at me. I didn't know if that was a friendly greeting or a warning to let me know he remembered me. The charge was read out to him. He was caught in possession of a rifle—how did he plead? He said, "Not guilty." The RM said the case would be heard in the Crown Court.

The third case was different. The defendant's father was a former pupil of mine. His son was in court because of non-attendance at school. This was the son's first appearance and social services were just asking for an adjournment so that they could prepare a report. So, I didn't have to withdraw. The solicitor had prepared a glowing report on the father: honest, reliable, hard-working, and completely committed to ensuring that his children were well-educated.

I wondered how well the solicitor knew the defendant's dad. To be fair, the father had never caused any problems in the school. That was because he was seldom at school. But he was one of the lucky ones. The attendance officer had never caught up with him. Had he changed his mind about education when it was too late for him and didn't want his son to make the same mistakes he had made? Hope springs eternal!

Some RMs could be described as fundamentalist in their religious beliefs, believing that children who committed serious offences are evil and should be punished severely for their crimes. They seem not to be aware that one of the tenets of Christianity, and of Islam, is that we should condemn the sin and not the sinner. I crossed swords with some of them on occasion.

On one occasion, we had a young man charged with stealing. The RM felt we should make a custodial order. I disagreed and argued for a probation order. The RM went along with that but there was a sting in the tail. He asked the young man to stand up and then announced our decision. He said to the defendant, "Hold out your hands. Those are the hands of a thief. You are a thief and will always be a thief." There was no room in the RM's mind for rehabilitation.

Some RMs appeared to be biased against certain members of society. I remember once a group of children were before the court charged with riotous behaviour in Belfast city centre the previous Saturday afternoon. It appeared that they were on their way home from a football match—Cliftonville v. Linfield. The Cliftonville supporters were mainly Catholic while the Linfield supporters were mainly Protestant. It was inevitable that when they met in the city centre, still wearing their team colours, fights would break out. A number were arrested and ended up before us in court on Monday morning. They were all charged with riotous behaviour. There were no serious injuries and no damage done to surrounding shops. None were identified as serial offenders. The obvious penalty was a conditional discharge.

The police presented no evidence as to which side started the fighting, but the RM had his own views. Before announcing the sentence, he lectured the Linfield supporters telling them that they should be ashamed of themselves for sullying the name of a good club. Then he 'tore into' the Cliftonville supporters. They were nothing but hooligans, not interested in football, just out to create havoc and ruin a day's enjoyment for everyone else.

On another occasion, we had a member of the traveller community before the court. The case was adjourned several times because the child failed to turn up. The RM held the father responsible and decided to make an example of him. I reminded him that we were a Juvenile Court and had no jurisdiction over adults. In any event, things didn't turn out quite as planned. A police officer gave evidence that he had delivered the summons to John Doe—the child's father. He insisted he had placed the summons directly in Mr Doe's hand. The RM said, "Would Mr John Doe please stand up?" Six men stood up and were able to present driving licences to show that they all were indeed named John Doe. The RM asked the police officer, "Which of these men did you hand the summons to?" The police officer had no idea. The case was dismissed.

When the regular RM was off, one of his colleagues would stand in. On one occasion, it was an RM who sat in the adult courts and had no experience in the Juvenile Court. We had to deal with a 12-year-old child charged with arson. The child, who was mitching school, had got in through the window of a vacant house and was having a smoke. For whatever reason, he set fire to the curtains. The ceiling caught fire and the fire spread through the roof space to the semi-detached house next door. A mother and her three young children who lived there had to be rescued by the fire service. The police initially contemplated charging the child with arson and attempted murder but decided to drop the 'attempted murder' charge.

The defence counsel pleaded 'Doli Incapax'. Under our law, a child less than ten years old cannot be held legally responsible for his or her actions, and so cannot be convicted of committing a criminal act. If their conduct would be seen as 'criminal' in a child over the age of ten, they must be dealt with by social services. At that time, there was a similar 'rebuttable presumption' that a child between the ages of ten and fourteen was not capable of committing a criminal offence. A 'rebuttable presumption' means that the prosecution would have to bring forward evidence to show that the child knew exactly what he/she was doing and knew that what they were doing was wrong. Usually, a psychologist or a psychiatrist would be asked to examine the child and advise the court as to whether the child should be held responsible for his/her actions. ('Doli Incapax' was abolished for children aged 10 to 14 by the *Crime and Disorder Act 1998*).

In this case, the psychologist asked the child whether he knew it was wrong to set fire to the curtains. The child said 'yes'—end of the interview. The RM said the prosecution had shown that the child knew what he was doing. I argued that it had not. Of course, the child knew it was wrong to set fire to the curtains. The prosecution had not shown that the child knew that the fire would spread to the ceiling and onwards through the roof space to the house next door, endangering the lives of the people living there. However, I was sitting alone with the RM, the female Lay Magistrate having failed to turn up. When there are only two on the Bench, and there is disagreement, the RM, as Chair, has the casting vote. He insisted that the case must proceed. There was only one possible outcome since the boy admitted to setting fire to the curtains. We made a finding of guilt.

At this point, the RM's lack of understanding of the Juvenile Court became obvious. He insisted that the penalties we could impose were insufficient in such a serious case and that we must send the child to the Crown Court for sentencing by a High Court judge. I advised him that we couldn't do that. He insisted that we must, as all serious cases are dealt with in the Crown Court. I tried to explain the rules governing the Juvenile Court. If we considered that the case was very serious (for example, if the charge of attempted murder had stood), we could refuse to hear it and have it transferred to the Crown Court. But, if we chose to hear it, as we had, then we must decide on the penalty. We could not transfer it to the Crown Court for sentencing. I pointed out that it was quite common for the Crown Court, on a finding of guilt, to send the child back to the Juvenile Court for sentencing on the grounds that we were more knowledgeable about the needs of the child than High Court judges.

The RM refused to accept my advice and had the casting vote. The case was transferred to the Crown Court. A few weeks later, I got a phone call from the RM asking if I could come in. He said that we had been rapped over the knuckles for sending the case to the Crown Court. It had been sent back and we now had to consider what sentence we should impose.

While all the most serious cases (like murder, or attempted murder) go automatically to the Crown Court, a child charged with a range of less serious offences can ask for a Crown Court trial. It is common practice for the RM, after reading out the charge, to ask the child whether he/she consents to the case being heard in the Juvenile Court. They consent in most cases. However, it is possible for the Bench to refuse to hear the case and to have it transferred to the Crown Court. Once, while sitting with the regular RM, a young man appeared charged with a serious sexual assault. The young woman had put up a fight, but he was a big lad, over 6 foot tall and he had given her a severe beating before sexually assaulting her. In normal circumstances, this case would have gone to the Crown Court. But unusually, the defence asked that we hear it. The prosecutor said he had no objections.

The RM and I retired to consider the options. We could agree and hear the case, or we could refuse and transfer it to the Crown Court. The maximum penalty we could normally impose was four years in the Young Offenders Centre. The Court of Appeal in England had recently ruled that the minimum sentence in the case of a serious assault and rape should be 14 years. If we agreed to hear this case, we would have to sentence the boy to at least 14 years. That would be setting a new precedent for the Juvenile Court. We didn't think that was a good idea. The RM ordered that the case be transferred.

My experiences sitting as a Lay Magistrate in the Youth Court and in the Family Proceedings Court proved invaluable in my new role training future teachers to work with troubled and troublesome young people. Taking into consideration my membership of the Board of Directors of one of our training schools, and my 13 years of experience working with these children in the school setting, it would be fair to say that I knew the system inside out. I used my knowledge of under-achieving early school-leavers to give my students an unforgettable glimpse of life for these children which I hoped would prepare them for their teaching career.

Chapter 17
Spreading the Word

Not for me the conveyor-belt approach of filling empty minds with knowledge. When I am in training mode, I remember the words of Kong Fuzi, better known under his Latinised name—Confucius, considered the paragon of Chinese sages.

What I hear, I forget. What I see, I remember. What I do, I understand.

When it comes to learning: hearing is not as good as seeing, seeing is not as good as experience, and true learning is only evident when experience produces an action.

I decided to explore with the students what happens to a typical child who makes a nuisance of him/herself in school. I explained that most children who got into difficulties in the classroom were male. In those days, the breakdown was 91% male and 9% female. We agreed that we would focus on boys behaving badly.

We discussed how the D-stream boys were turned off school by the time they got to their final year. What happened to those who decided not to attend? Some stayed at home, their absence condoned by their parents. Some found casual work, perhaps in pubs cleaning up the debris of late-night drinking. Others simply spent their day 'dossing about'.

Not all the young people mitching[28] school were likely to end up in court—the attendance officers were never that efficient. But persistent offenders who did end up in court were liable to receive a sentence of '1 to 3 Years' in a training school. '1 to 3 Years' meant that they would have to stay in the training school for a minimum of one year and a maximum of three. The release date would be determined by the progress they made.

There were two topics of debate here. The first was the issue of detention for children who were not attending school and the second was 'indeterminate sentencing' which meant that there was no fixed date for release.

In those days, there were large numbers of children receiving training school orders for mitching school. Indeed, non-attendance cases made up the bulk of cases passing through the juvenile courts. I, and others, had demonstrated that the school curriculum and teaching methods had a major role to play in non-attendance. There was a growing groundswell of opinion that schools should be 'consuming their own smoke'. If schools made the curriculum meaningful for children, children would attend. The authorities were not listening. It was many years before change was introduced.

Indeterminate sentencing was also the subject of heated debate. The child would be told simply that he/she had received a '1–3 Year Training School Order'. On arrival at the relevant training school, they would be told that, if they

---

[28] *Mitching* or *Truanting* means absenting themselves from school without permission.

behaved and got on well with staff they would be detained for the minimum period. If not, they could be in for the full term. This meant that the period of detention was left to the discretion of the staff. If the staff, for whatever reason, took umbrage against a child, that child could be detained for the full three years. Many of us considered it not just unfair, but unjust that a child should be sentenced to a period of detention but given no indication as to how long that period might be. Again, it would be many years before those of us who were lobbying for change succeeded in having it replaced with fixed periods of detention.

Those children not attending school who spent their days 'dossing about' were liable to get themselves into further trouble by getting involved in criminal activity—shoplifting for example. If apprehended the penalty was likely to be the same—a 1- to 3-year detention order.

As noted above, we followed some of these children through the court. The students had an opportunity to meet with a resident magistrate and two lay colleagues in Chambers after the court session finished to discuss the day's hearings. The students were able to discuss individual cases and talk about the penalties.

The next step was to visit the boys in one of the training schools. At that time, the training schools dealt with three categories of children: a) children who were deemed to be in need of care and protection and who had been placed there by the courts under a care order; b) children who were in conflict with the law and who had received a sentence of '1 to 3' years for their offending behaviour and c) children who refused to attend school and had been sentenced to '1 to 3' years for mitching. Children on Care Orders were kept separate from offenders, but they all shared the same campus. The students focused on those children who were in the training school because of their failure to attend school.

I wanted the students to learn that the children who mitch school, or who are in conflict with the law, are normal children who require additional support and understanding, not detention. Some might have physical or mental health problems. For many, their problems originated in a troubled home background. I hoped that, in following my course, the students would learn how to keep these children in mainstream schools and cut the numbers ending up in institutions.

The 1944 Education Act confirmed youth work provision as directed at young people in their leisure hours. Youth work was seen as being totally separated from schooling since youth work is based on relationships which are voluntarily entered into, while schooling is compulsory. In short, youth work is relationship-focused and schooling is curriculum-driven.

Mindful of the need to strike a balance between learning, practising, and doing, I asked the students to agree to a youth club placement at least one night per week. I placed them in youth clubs rather than schools because the element of compulsion was removed. The young people did not have to attend the youth club. They could walk out if they did not like the youth leader or what he/she was offering. The youth leader had to offer an attractive programme to get the young people to come to the club in the first instance and then depend on the force of his/her personality to keep them there.

I wanted the students to learn informal teaching techniques. They would have the opportunity to put theory into practice. They would learn new skills by observing the youth workers. They would learn the importance of building good relationships with young people and using personal influence and respect to guide behaviour. The students loved the youth club work, and most were working additional nights helping out.

It was important also to try to identify how the young people had got onto the slippery slope in the first place and what might have been done to prevent them from going down this route and ending up in training school.

Arising from the youth club placements, we identified a group of hard-core *mitchers*—children who had not been to school for a long time. Most had spent periods in St Patrick's but had not returned to full-time education on release. We invited these children to work with us. We got permission from the college principal to bring them into the college once per week so that the students could work with them either individually or collectively. The intention was to identify why they had given up on school, what their problems were, what would make them go back to school and what help or support they required.

The students learned a lot from the boys. They learned that, in the case of this group, the bad reputation was deserved since they were all into petty crime, including joyriding. And yet these were good lads—pleasant, mannerly, and easy to work with.

Two key points the students learned were that when trying to find out why a child is falling behind: 1) it is important not to ignore the obvious and 2) early intervention is critical. What a different outcome there might have been for the boys in our group had the teachers spotted the obvious in the early days! Simply moving the child who could not see the board properly, or the one who could not hear, to the front of the class (pending a medical referral) might have made such a difference. A little bit of additional support for the young man who had difficulty keeping up might have worked wonders. Ignoring the obvious and branding the boys as stupid and lazy could have tragic consequences for some children.

Chapter 18
No Escaping the Troubles

Unfortunately, tragedy was all too common, not only in the lives of young people in St Peter's but also in the lives of children throughout Northern Ireland as the guerrilla war got bloodier by the day.

When I first arrived in Belfast in 1957, many people from the Falls Road would shop on the Shankill Road. They believed that there was a better range of shops and that it was possible to get better quality goods at lower prices than on the Falls Road or in the city centre. Saturday morning was always particularly busy on the Shankill.

The love of shopping on the Shankill vanished like snow off a ditch following the attack by Protestant paramilitaries and B-Specials on Catholics in the Falls Road area of West Belfast on 14 and 15 August 1969. These attacks impacted like an earthquake, opening a wide chasm between the Falls and the Shankill. The Falls Road residents were happy to see the streets linking the two permanently closed by the British army. A few streets were left open during the day to allow access for necessary vehicular traffic but closed at night.

The chasm between the Falls and the Shankill got even wider when 'The Shankill Butchers' started their anti-

Catholic campaign. The Shankill Butchers was the name given to a Protestant paramilitary gang based on the Shankill Road which was active between 1975 and 1982. Many of the gang members were also members of the Ulster Volunteer Force (UVF).

The gang was notorious for kidnapping, torturing, and murdering random Catholics or suspected Catholics. Three or four gang members would drive around a Catholic area in a taxi in the early hours of the morning looking for a Catholic walking alone. They would jump out, bundle that person into the taxi and bring him/her to a house on the Shankill Road. There they would receive a horrific beating, be slashed with knives or broken bottles, attacked with a hatchet, and finally have their throat slit with a butcher's knife. The nature of some of the wounds, which were too horrific to describe here, led the police to believe that one or more of the gang members had experience of working in an abattoir. Hence, the name given to the gang. When they were finished, the body dumped bore little resemblance to the person kidnapped and bundled into the taxi.

In their seven-year reign of terror, the gang killed 23 Catholics. They also killed six Protestants who were involved in personal disputes with one or more gang members and two other Protestants who had been mistaken for Catholics.

I was surprised therefore when the youth officer responsible for training in the Belfast Education and Library Board invited me to run a counselling course for the board's full-time youth workers. The course would be held in the Hammer Youth Club on the Shankill Road in Belfast.

Bearing in mind what I said above, you might have expected to hear a resounding, 'No way'. But there were other things to consider. The youth officer with responsibility for training was a very good friend of mine. He was a Catholic, as were about 50% of the youth workers. If they felt it was safe to attend a course in the Hammer Youth Club, why shouldn't I? Besides, the course would be held in the early afternoon. I agreed to teach the course which we all completed without incident.

One day, at the beginning of October 1979, I was driving up the Falls Road on my way back to Trench House from St Mary's. As I approached the zebra crossing just before the junction with Whiterock Road, a man stepped onto the crossing and stood right in front of my car with his back to me. As I jammed on the brakes, I noticed that he had a revolver in his right hand. I then saw a second gunman step out of the gates of the City Cemetery diagonally opposite. Just with that, both men opened fire on a car coming down Whiterock Road. They clearly hit their target as the car stopped for a few seconds and then careered across the road in front of me, crashing into the railings at the top of St James's Road to my left. The doors burst open, and I could see that the driver had collapsed onto the passenger seat.

I had no way of knowing who the gunmen were or who the victim was. I didn't stop to think. I jumped out of the car and ran to the victim's aid. I thought he was already dead but decided to raise his head and whisper an Act of Contrition in his ear. I slipped my left hand under his shoulder and my right hand around the back of his head. To my horror, I discovered that the back of his head was gone. My hand was covered in thick, thick blood. Later as I tried to wash my hands, I found it very difficult to get rid of the feel of the blood, while the smell of the blood persisted for a long, long time. But at that moment I was focused on prayer.

As I knelt there, I sensed someone behind me. I looked up to find a man reaching over my shoulder. He didn't speak to me. He just reached into the back and retrieved two rifles. He walked back across the top of St James's Road and merged into a crowd which had now assembled there. I hadn't noticed the spectators gathering. The situation was now clear to me. This had been an IRA ambush, and I assumed, the occupants of the car had been undercover soldiers. There were two rifles but only one victim. Where was the other occupant? I would later learn that he had somehow managed to get out of the car during the few seconds the car was stopped and race back up the hill towards Fort Pegasus to raise the alarm. I could only imagine that the driver had stood on the brakes as the ambush was sprung and the passenger had taken the opportunity to jump out. When the driver was shot his foot slipped off the brake and the car careered across the road.

This was just after Pope John Paul II's visit to Ireland, in 1979. In a direct address to the consciences of both terrorists and politicians on his visit to Drogheda on 29 September, he said, "On my knees, I beg you to turn away from the paths of violence and return to the ways of peace." The visit was beamed live to churches in Northern Ireland, including St John's Church on the Falls Road, about 50 yards from where this shooting occurred. The congregation burst into loud applause on hearing the pope's words on 29 September. Now, just a few days later, here was part of that congregation, less than 50 yards from St John's Church, applauding the murder of an undercover soldier and urging the gunmen to get offside before the police and the army arrived.

I thought that my own life could well be in danger as I saw the crowd watching me assisting 'the enemy'. But I was too angry to care. I decided to wait for the police and army to arrive and to make a statement of what I had seen of the incident. Once I had done that, I got into my car and headed for Trench House where I tried to remove the blood stains and get back to 'normal' life.

The early 1980s was an exciting time in the youth and community field. I was working flat out on a range of projects when I was approached by the chief inspector of schools and offered a job in the inspectorate. He was aware of the work I had done with persistent 'mitchers' and wanted me to develop a programme for teachers on dealing with disaffected pupils to cut the non-attendance rate.

I explained to him that my wife had a terminal illness and needed care 24/7. Trench House was just a few minutes' walk for me, and I could nip home for lunch each day. If I was needed urgently, I could be home in minutes. If I had to miss a lecture, I could arrange another time with the students. As an inspector, I would have youth clubs to visit in various parts of Northern Ireland, and this would require me to be away from home frequently in the evenings. I didn't have any outside help or support at night. Unfortunately, the only option I had was to say, 'No'.

In 1984, I was surprised when the principal called me into his office to tell me that the youth and community course was to be discontinued. He said that there had been a directive from the Department of Education that the teacher-training colleges should henceforth concentrate on preparing teachers for primary schools. Since the youth and community course was aimed at secondary teachers, it would no longer be offered. I drew his attention to some of the children we had worked with and said that if work with them had begun in primary school the outcome would have been different. In my view, a course aimed at 'working with difficult children' was very relevant to primary teachers. The principal's response was that a decision had been taken. I would be offered the option of switching to computer studies and would be given a year's study leave so that I could attend a course at Queen's University. I had no interest in teaching computer studies. But my wife had to get priority. I said I would take the course.

In 1984, Trench House merged with St Mary's on the Falls Road site. This was my new base when I completed the course in Queen's at the end of the 1984/85 academic year. Once I got started lecturing again, the students soon won me over. Many of them had never used a computer before and some of them were terrified at the thought of having to learn a skill which was alien to them. Considering my own experience, it was easy for me to empathise with them. I could appreciate their panic when the computer wouldn't work. Instead of labelling them as stupid, I would advise them to start with the basics. Is the computer plugged in? Is it switched on? Is the disc in the drive?

My new role was very different from my youth and community work, but I was still working with students and living up to my own ideals of helping them to be the best they could be. The academic year 1985/86 passed quickly. And then, in the summer of 1986, my life changed dramatically when my wife Bernie died. Her death was totally unexpected, even though the doctors had told me on at least five occasions over the previous few years, "She will not come out of this—it is only a matter of time." We arrived home from a holiday in Cyprus and Egypt on Friday, 11 July. Liam spent all of Saturday sitting on her bed, looking through holiday brochures with her and planning our next holiday. She had a massive stroke in the early hours of Sunday morning. She died in my arms on Wednesday, 16 July 1986.

Liam and I were not the only people grieving. The Troubles were still at their height and death was all around us. On Sunday morning, 14 September 1986, we had just got in from Mass when I heard a volley of shots and then screaming just in front of my house. I ran out and saw a young man lying, face down, in a pool of blood about 20 yards from my front gate. I was about to run down to see if I could offer any help when a group of soldiers came running across the road screaming at me to keep away. They claimed he was a terrorist whom they had been trying to capture. I had no way of knowing. I saw no gun and noted that he had been shot in the back. Years later, a plaque was erected on my neighbour's wall close to the spot where he had been shot, naming him as an IRA volunteer.

Tension was higher than normal in West Belfast early in 1988 because of a heavy security presence at several high-profile Irish republican funerals. Police tactics were criticised as instigating unrest, leading the authorities to adopt a 'hands-off' policy with respect to policing IRA funerals.

On 6 March 1988, members of the Special Air Service shot and killed three unarmed IRA members who were, allegedly, preparing for a bomb attack on the band of the Royal Anglian Regiment in Gibraltar. Their unpoliced funeral along the Falls Road to Milltown Cemetery, on 16 March, was attacked by Michael Stone, a member of the Protestant paramilitary Ulster Defence Association. Three people were killed and more than 60 wounded as he opened fire and lobbed hand grenades into the crowd. One of the dead was an IRA volunteer. The atmosphere at this IRA man's funeral, held three days later was extremely tense, with everyone expecting another loyalist attack. When two out-of-uniform soldiers were spotted observing the funeral the crowd attacked the soldiers' car. The soldiers were dragged out and shot dead about one hundred yards down the road from where I live.

The authorities insisted that the two soldiers, both corporals, drove into the funeral accidentally. I find it hard to believe that army intelligence was not aware of the funeral. The murder of the two corporals was fully captured by television cameras and has been described as one of the 'most dramatic and harrowing images' of The Troubles.

On 13 January 1990, three men were controversially killed by a top-secret army intelligence unit as they carried out a robbery at a bookmaker's, at the bottom of Whiterock Road in West Belfast. The first man, who was unarmed, was shot ten times as he emerged from the bookies. The second, who was carrying a concealed weapon in his clothing, was hit 12 times—nine of those in the back. The getaway driver was shot in the face at point-blank range while sitting behind the wheel of a car waiting for the others to emerge.

It was alleged that this army unit had their car stolen by joyriders some weeks before. The joyriders passed sports bags containing guns and highly confidential army papers to the three men involved in the raid on the bookies. The police had already retrieved all the material. There were claims the killings could have been a pre-planned 'shoot to kill' revenge attack for embarrassing the security force's most elite unit. The soldiers were not prosecuted, and no enquiry was held.

Terrorist-related activity continued almost daily. It was 'normal' to have to skirt around the burnt-out remains of buses, lorries, and cars—the debris of the previous night's rioting—or to make detours to avoid suspect bombs on the way to and from work. The most disconcerting aspect for me was that death and destruction became so commonplace that incidents were quickly forgotten apart from the more horrific ones like those noted above.

Chapter 19
It Just Grow'd

Dicing with Death provides a frank and honest insight into my life and career living and working in the unique environment of West Belfast throughout a prolonged period of guerrilla warfare. I sometimes find it hard to believe what I achieved considering the war raging around me. But, strange as it may seem, this is only half of the story. A campaign to promote the rights of disaffected children in St Peter's Secondary School in West Belfast became a regional campaign to promote the rights of disaffected children in schools across Northern Ireland before becoming a national, and later an international, worldwide, campaign for the rights of all children. How did this happen? The response which springs to mind is that of Rudyard Kipling in 1885, explaining to a correspondent that, "I have really embarked...on my novel. Like Topsy 'it grow'd' while I wrote." Like Topsy, I would answer, 'It just grow'd'[29].

---

[29] **Uncle Tom's Cabin** or, *Life Among the Lowly* is an anti-slavery novel by American author Harriet Beecher Stowe. Published in two volumes in 1852. In *Uncle Tom's Cabin*, Topsy is being questioned about her parents by Ophilia and replies, "Don't think nobody never

Let me reflect briefly on the life journey that brought me here.

My two mentors (my dad and my primary school principal—Master Sheeran) instilled in me, in my early years, the values of honesty, hard work, a commitment to education and an unshakeable belief that if I worked hard and lived responsibly, I could achieve anything I put my mind to. I applied most scrupulously the message learned and it has shaped my life. The leitmotiv of my existence is *I am the master of my fate: I am the captain of my soul*[30].

I chose teaching as a career because I wanted to help under-achievers carve out a better future for themselves. When I started teaching, colleagues said I had a gift for getting my message across to young people. But it is not a 'gift'. The 'secret' is respect. I respected the pupils, and they respected me. As a rule, they listened when I spoke to them.

My aim was to help under-achievers develop self-confidence, a belief in themselves and a belief that they have innate talents which could be developed. I wanted them to believe that they could achieve something better if they put their minds to it.

I believe that the correct way to educate children is not through the learning of lessons by heart in a servile way, but by using their critical faculties, going beyond school textbooks towards the reality of situations and the complexity of daily events.

---

made me. I spect I grow'd." Soon 'it grow'd like Topsy' became a popular figure of speech to describe something that grew or increased by itself, without apparent design or intention.

[30] *Invictus*-W E Henley.

I developed my own philosophy of education, rooted in the classical approach but firmly grounded in my experience. I believe that every child should be given the chance to be educated to the limit of his/her talents. I accept that not every child has an equal talent or an equal ability or an equal motivation, but they all have an equal right to develop what talent they have, to make something of themselves. It is the role of the school to ensure that every child has a fair chance to succeed and to go as far and as high as their talent and willingness to work will take them. A school's success should not be measured solely by the number of children achieving O-levels and A-levels. Success should be measured by the extent to which the teachers help all children develop their talents to the maximum.

I was convinced that having someone who believed in him/her could explain why a child succeeds when everyone is expecting failure. The 'someone' doesn't have to be a family member. When the child comes from a dysfunctional family, a grandparent, youth worker, priest, friend or teacher could take that role. In any event, the teacher will play a key role since he/she knows what the child is capable of and is in the best position to help the child develop his/her hidden talents.

That doesn't mean that they should accept whatever the child does. I would always demand high standards and would not accept shoddy work. If the work isn't done properly, it has to be done again. I would always remind them that 'if the job is worth doing, it is worth doing well'. If they didn't get it right the first time, they should be given an opportunity to do it again until they get it right. I would promise that there would be no red biro marks in the finished product.

Higher education changed everything for me. It is not for everyone, but it should be readily available for those who want it. No one can be guaranteed success, but everyone should have a fair chance to succeed.

In *Dicing with Death*, my focus has been on the rights of under-achieving children in schools. However, when I listed the various agencies that I was involved with, I was highlighting that children have the same rights as adults and my goal was to ensure that I was campaigning on their behalf for all rights to be guaranteed.

I have written a lengthy chapter on my work as a Lay Magistrate and a Justice of the Peace because that is where I had the most opportunities to defend children's rights. I felt that my fellow magistrates would pay more attention to what I said if I were one of them.

I was Chair of the Northern Ireland Intermediate Treatment Association, which developed projects to keep young offenders out of custody. I was a member of the Probation Board for Northern Ireland which offered alternatives to custody.

I was Chair of Glenand Youth and Community Workshop which catered for those young people who left school at the first opportunity without qualifications, Vice-Chair of Worknet (Falls Development Agency) which fulfilled a similar role, and Chair of the Greater Suffolk Research and Study Project. The belief was that if young people could learn a trade and find a job, they were less likely to get in trouble with the law.

As a group work advisor to the Belfast Education and Library Board and to Dublin's Vocational Education Committee, I provided training for full-time youth workers. I was a consultant to the Northern Ireland Youth Council Research Project.

Where the young offender is a danger to him/herself or to members of the community, there may be no alternative to custody. Still, I believe in the resilience of children. The focus should be on reintegrating him/her back into the community. Planning for their release should ideally start as soon as they begin their custodial sentence so that the services and the support they need are available when and where they need them. I joined the Board of Directors of St Patrick's Training School to monitor what plans were put in place.

During my 13-year teaching career, I demonstrated that when the pupils sensed a positive attitude on the part of the teacher and were given an opportunity to feel good about themselves, they responded positively. I wanted to provide teachers with an incentive to encourage their pupils to work instead of resorting to punishment for not working. If the teacher respected the pupils, the pupils would respect him/her. Respect is the key to success.

While I got very positive results from the pupils, I couldn't say the same for teachers. They didn't believe that they had any role to play in changing the curriculum. They insisted that it was up to the pupils to change their approach to learning. It was not up to the teachers to change their teaching methods.

I came to realise that the teachers were set in their ways. The way forward was to sell my ideas to student teachers before they began their teaching careers and before they could develop bad habits. I applied for a post in St Joseph's (Trench House) and was appointed Head of Youth and Community

Work. I was about to widen my campaign to cover all of Northern Ireland.

My aim was to have 10 to 20 teachers leaving the college each year who would put my theories into practice. As time passed, a growing number of newly qualified teachers would welcome the challenge of working with the D-streams and helping the young people be the best they could be.

After 21 years of teacher training, former students were scattered around Northern Ireland, some in schools, some in youth clubs, some in special schools and some in voluntary organisations. Some have taken things to a higher level with Doctorates and Masters. One became the principal of a special school. One is working for the Northern Ireland Court Service writing reports on families due to appear before the Family Proceedings Court. One became the director of a large voluntary organisation which prepares young people from dysfunctional families for the world of work. Two were appointed as inspectors for the Northern Ireland Youth Service. I couldn't ask for more.

I developed my philosophy of education during my 13 years of teaching, and the programme I prepared for my students when I moved to Trench House in 1974 was based on it. My philosophy struck a discordant note with my colleagues in Trench House and with teachers in general in Northern Ireland. It appeared that I was ahead of my time. My approach struck a chord on the international scene, and I received invitations from different parts of the world to present papers on my work. My campaign became international, and I was travelling around the globe.

The United Nations Convention on the Rights of the Child (UNCRC) was adopted by the UN General Assembly and opened for signature on 20 November 1989. It came into force on 12 September 1990, after it was ratified by the required number of nations. It was the first legally binding international instrument to incorporate the full range of human rights for children and the most ratified in the history of the UN. 196 countries are party to it, including every member of the United Nations, except the United States. It has a total of 54 articles. No article is regarded as more important than any other. But there are four that are seen as special. They are known as the 'Guiding Principles' and they play a fundamental role in realising all the rights in the Convention for all children. They are Non-Discrimination (Article 2); the Best Interests of the Child (Article 3); the Right to Life, Survival and Development (Article 6); Respect for the Views of the Child (Article 12).

As I read the UNCRC, I was drawn to the four 'Guiding Principles'. It was reassuring to note that three of the four could have been taken directly from my philosophy of education. Article 6 does not fall within the remit of teachers per se, but for teachers like me, who were caught up in Northern Ireland's urban guerrilla war, it could be argued that it is a key article.

Now I knew why there was so much interest in my philosophy of education when I began testing it in 1974. I was on the same wavelength as those working on the UNCRC. In my 21 years in Trench House, I had invitations to Argentina, Brazil, Canada, China, England, Italy, Mexico, Scotland, and Switzerland. I had five different trips to the USA with visits to 20 US states in total. Most of these international trips were after 1986 with a steep rise following the coming into force of the UNCRC on 2 September 1990.

In 1986, I took one small unremarkable step forward when I became more active in the Northern Ireland Lay Magistrates Association (NILMA). I was elected Honorary Secretary of NILMA in 1982 and served in this post for 8 years the longest period served by anyone before or since. The association had a newsletter—a small, A-5-sized booklet published twice yearly. It carried items of interest, and gossip, submitted by members. I took over as editor in 1982 and turned it into a 36-page (A-4 sized) magazine which was much more of an educational tool. It carried articles focussing on child development, child welfare and how best to deal with offending behaviour—in short, articles which would help Lay Magistrates better understand the complexities of the cases they faced in court. I remained as editor for 26 years.

I had not expected that one of my responsibilities as Honorary Secretary was to be the Northern Ireland representative on the executive committee of the British Juvenile and Family Court Society (BJFCS). A small step of accepting the role of Honorary Secretary of NILMA became a giant stride into the BJFCS when I discovered that I had five or six trips to London per year.

Even then I did not expect to be elected Chair of the BJFCS in 1990 for a three-year period, the only Irish person to ever hold that post. I edited their magazine from 1990 to 1998. I was elected Chair of the Northern Ireland Association in 1992. So, I found myself chairing both associations at the same time—a unique experience.

Arising from my election as Chair of the BJFCS, I was elected to the General Purposes Committee of the International Association of Youth and Family Judges and Magistrates (IAYFJM) at their World Congress in Turin in

1990. I was appointed Editor-in-Chief of the Chronicle, the magazine of the IAYFJM, at a meeting in London in 1991. The Chronicle is published twice a year in English, French and Spanish. I was elected to the 20-member Council of the IAYFJM at the World Congress in Bremen, Germany in August 1994. I was elected Vice President of the IAYFJM at the World Congress in Buenos Aires in 1998 and President of the IAYFJM at the World Congress in Melbourne, Australia in 2002.

By 1995, I was regarded as an expert on children's rights and my services were in demand, not only by many governments but also by organisations such as the UN Development Programme, the Council of Europe and UNICEF. There was a continuous flow of requests for me to get involved in a range of projects as well as requests from various countries to present papers at seminars.

I was satisfied that I had achieved my objective of having a team of teachers and youth workers across Northern Ireland helping children and young people to be the best they could be. My philosophy was in good hands. I could do no more on the local scene since my course had been stopped. I got an opportunity to apply for early retirement. I accepted the offer. I retired at the end of August 1995 after 13 years of teaching followed by 21 years of training teachers. I was 57. The stream of requests to get involved in international projects became a flood. There was no question of sitting back and enjoying retirement. I had to bring my theories to a wider audience.

I hope that readers will understand now why, like Topsy, I said, 'It just grow'd'. The small step which I took to promote the rights of disaffected children in St Peter's Secondary

School in West Belfast grew or increased by itself, without any design or intention on my part, into an international, worldwide, campaign for the rights of all children.

Who would have thought that someone with my background would embark on a national, regional, and later international campaign to promote the rights of children? How could anyone have imagined that becoming a member of NILMA would prove to be the first rung of the ladder which I would climb to become Chair of NILMA, Chair of the BJFCS and President of the IAYFJM?

Who could have imagined that I would one day be invited to fly to Buenos Aires to advise their Council of Judges on how to solve a very confidential and very delicate issue which was threatening to split the council in half?

Who would have guessed that I would have to fly to Melbourne to advise the executive of their judicial council regarding what should be prioritised when it looked like the cost of hosting the World Congress would exceed the sponsorship?

When the Chinese government was concerned about international criticism of its use of the death penalty[31] who would have imagined that I would be invited to go for a walk on the Great Wall (where we were out of range of would-be eavesdroppers) to be told of a proposal to reduce the number of executions by 20%? Who would have guessed that they would seek my views on whether the proposal would be welcomed by human rights organisations and by the UN? I

---

[31] There had been a steep rise in the number of executions in China, which was already sentencing more people to death for a range of offences than most other nations in the world taken together.

would never even have dreamt that I would be strolling along the Great Wall of China discussing such an important human rights issue.

No one could possibly have foreseen any of this. It all seemed like a dream to me.

How can anyone understand my life journey which led me to so many of the world's countries? The key to understanding rests with my two mentors who instilled in me the unshakeable belief that with dedication, application, and hard work I could achieve anything I put my mind to.

But the main driver, which would not have been obvious to them at the time, was my permanent enthusiasm for the cause of the youngest members of society.

People often ask how many talks have I given. How many articles have I written? How many seminars have I chaired? How many young professionals have I helped? I tell them I don't know. I don't keep such statistics, but I can give some examples of things I remember.

I took a group of disaffected young people on a day trip to the Mountains of Mourne, Northern Ireland's highest mountain range. I parked the minibus beside the Silent Valley Reservoir and told them they could go for a walk while I heated a pot of soup for their lunch. When I went out to call them, I could hear their voices echoing around Silent Valley, 'Wee Willie's OK!' I put that down as a vote of confidence in my teaching skills.

I was giving a talk to a large mixed group of practitioners in the University of Ulster. A young man came up to me and said he had first heard me speak at a conference at Sterling University, in Scotland, some ten years previous. He had been so impressed that he decided to train as a social worker. He was delighted that he had taken that decision and he wanted to thank me.

I was taking a judicial training programme in Tajikistan when one of the judges approached me during the coffee break. She said that she had attended a training programme I had taken there eight years before. She told me that she had learned a lot from the course and had subsequently been promoted to the Supreme Court. When she heard I was back again running another course, she immediately applied to attend. She said she was sure she would learn a lot from this course too.

These kinds of comments are extremely useful as they help to reassure me that I am on the right track.

In trying to answer how a campaign to promote the rights of disaffected children in St Peter's Secondary School in West Belfast became a worldwide campaign for the rights of all children, I turn to my capacity for hard work, my determination, and my conviction. My faith in children never wavers. Even on occasions when I had doubts, my internal strength and my passion have always been stronger.

I hope that I have set an example which others might follow. I trust that this account encourages young people to commit to investing their skills in the service of defending children's rights.

I began with some details about the trials that life imposed on me and the way I overcame them. I gave you a glimpse of life roaming the world as a champion of children's rights—a global campaign for more justice for the weakest, youngest and most vulnerable among us: children. I spent my life defending children in the many different positions I have occupied and the numerous responsibilities I have taken on.

While my focus in *Dicing with Death* was on schools, I was helping children and young people in a range of situations. I dedicated my vision, my values, and my convictions to the cause of a fairer justice system for young people. I called for a justice system which distances itself from retribution in favour of proportionate social responses, adapted to the age and maturity of young offenders and especially one which gives them a second chance. I called for alternatives to the deprivation of liberty.

The urban guerrilla war in Northern Ireland has ended but the struggle for children's rights continues, not just in Northern Ireland but all around the world. Despite the energy, faith, the devotion which I brought, and continue to bring, to these many endeavours, I know that my efforts alone will not change the world. Sometimes I grew tired, thinking of the millions of children who needed help and considering how little I could do. Then I reminded myself of the story about a severe storm which stranded thousands of starfish on a beach. A man watched a little boy walking along the beach picking them up one by one and tossing them into the sea. He went up to the boy and asked him what he was doing. The boy explained that he was trying to save the starfish.

The man replied, "There are thousands of them. The few you save will make no difference."

The boy bent down, picked up another starfish and threw it into the sea. He turned to the man and said, "It made a difference to that one!"

I am encouraged by the words of Robert Kennedy:

Each time a man stands up for an ideal, or acts to improve the lot of others, or strikes out against injustice, he sends forth a tiny ripple of hope, and, crossing each other from a million different centres of energy and daring, those ripples build a current which can sweep down the mightiest walls of oppression and resistance.

There is no escaping the fact that the work of promoting the best interests of children is a seemingly never-ending struggle which requires perseverance, faith and understanding.

Still, I am reassured by the words of Mother Teresa: *God doesn't require us to succeed. He only requires that we try.*

In 2011, I organised a judicial training programme in one of Turkmenistan's five provinces. In 2012, I organised two more programmes. I was to complete the training in the remaining two provinces in 2013. However, the Turkmen government was in dispute with UNICEF and the training was cancelled.

I was diagnosed with Parkinson's Disease in January 2014 and some months later was told that I needed to go into the hospital for a quintuple (heart) bypass. I was advised to give up long-haul international flights. I thought that, at 74, I was too young to retire. I talked it over with my sister, Una. We decided that the next chapter would be sponsored walks to raise money for research into Parkinson's Disease. We have taken part in every sponsored walk since.

I will be 86 in four months' time (31 August 2024). But I am not giving up yet. The next walk will be on 20 October— six weeks after my 86th birthday. I am already registered for it. I still get occasional requests to give talks locally, two in the last couple of months. The money raised went towards Parkinson's research. It looks like I have a pretty light schedule for the months ahead. But who knows what tomorrow brings?